THE COSMIC CHRIST

*New Prayers and Prophecies
from Mother Mary*

TAMBOR SOLANA

BLUE COUGAR
P R E S S

SAN RAFAEL, CALIFORNIA

Ave Maria

THE COSMIC CHRIST

New Prayers and Prophecies
from Mother Mary

Front cover: collage includes a reverse image of a portion of
Botticelli's *Madonna del libro* (c. 1480).

CONTENTS

INTRODUCTION
I Am Not the Author

I work sometimes as a spiritual healer. People have asked me who does the healing on these occasions. I know that if I don't show up, the healing doesn't occur, so I must be an integral part of the equation. However, Spirit takes many forms, and these different forms show up at different times for different healings. So what is the correct answer to the question, "Who does the healing?" In a way it is the same as the answer to the question, "Who wrote this book?"

Sometime in April 1996, my friend Lia told my friend Shelley of a premonition that I would be teaching a course on the coming of the Cosmic Christ. The week after Shelley informed me of this conversation, while in meditation, I had a vision of Mother Mary. She told me I was not giving Her enough attention lately. It was true. My focus had been on other spiritual practices, mostly Tibetan Buddhist. I felt humbled, but willing to be open and to serve Her. I gathered Shelley and Lia and other friends and announced that I would facilitate a six-week course on the coming of the Cosmic Christ. It would be given by Mother Mary.

On the evening of May 7, 1996, we gathered in a small circle and began our first session. Shelley and her daughter had made a beautiful little altar in the middle of the circle with many fresh flowers, candles, and a picture of Mother Mary. I turned on the tape recorder, and Mother Mary appeared to me, with my eyes open, about fifteen to twenty feet away. She spoke to me, and I in turn spoke Her words to those present at the circle.

This brings up the whole subject of "channeling," a word used to describe the process whereby a person becomes a medium for voices from other dimensions to speak through. There are many kinds of channelers. Some people fall into a complete trance when they channel and don't remember anything they said. Others have a partial memory, while still others have total memory. There are a few serious issues involved with channeling, even if you readily accept it as a factual phenomenon.

The first problem has to do with the source of the messages. This is especially the case with trance-channelers who are unconscious of the process they are involved in. (However, perhaps the greatest of all twentieth-century American channelers, Edgar Cayce, was a traditional full-trance channel.) To add to the confusion, a trance-channeler might be channeling different sources at different times without knowing it.

The second problem has to do with the preparation and capacity of the channeler to bodily conduct the vibrations associated with the messages. Sometimes the frequencies associated with certain messages are so intense that the information reported is a little suspect. Also, there can be health problems associated with prolonged channeling work, even leading to premature death.

A true clairvoyant can "see" the guide that someone is channeling. I have observed channelers that I knew were fakes, because there were no guides present. Their information was totally unverifiable and there was not much of a spiritual feeling. It was salesmanship —a great act, and often a lucrative one. I have also seen guides who were totally hoodwinking their medium and the medium's audience, as if they were thinking, "Is it possible that this group would believe this load of malarkey?" Sure enough, the audience would fawn over every utterance, much to the delight of the mischievous guides. I have seen some popular channeled books that to me represent the same trickery.

Certain types of minerals have been referred to as "fool's gold," because they look like gold and have been passed off to the unsuspecting as gold. However, there can be no "fool's gold" without *real* gold with which to confuse it. Real gold is immensely valuable —a real treasure. You just need to be able to tell the difference between the two.

For me, this book is real gold.

I wish to say a word about the guides who speak in this book. Whenever Mother Mary is talking, I am not acting as a typical channeler. I am seeing Her and listening to Her, fully conscious, and with open eyes. I am repeating what She is telling me. She is the source of Her communications to me.

When Sanat Kumar speaks, it is a process similar to that with Mother Mary. I see him, and I repeat to the group what he says to me. It is different with the voices of the Archangels, however. When they are speaking, it appears much more like a conscious channeling session. I am not seeing them like I see Mother Mary. I am speaking their words like a medium.

Two aspects of this work deserve special mention. The first is that this book primarily represents an oral teaching. Sometimes a teaching, or "dharma" as it is often called in Eastern traditions, is oral and sometimes it is written. The difference is important because oral teachings are useful to bring spiritual energy to the throat of the speaker of the teachings, and spiritual energy not only to the mind of the listener but to the ears as well. Written teachings, on the other hand, specifically bring spiritual energy to the mind of the reader. I urge the audience of this book *to read the text out loud, alone or to one another,* instead of reading it silently. Because this dharma was transmitted orally, it can be compared to a screenplay which is much better presented when read aloud than when read silently.

Second, this work is infused with spiritual vibration and spiritual activation. Frequently, spiritual activations were bestowed on those present during the original presentations of the material. Thus, **these discourses are not merely verbal information.** Mother Mary specifically criticizes theology for forgetting the vibration of the "feeling" associated with dharma. She talks about "vibrational knowledge," which I feel is a beautiful and concise description of what wisdom is versus what knowledge is. True dharma has a vibration to it. It is beautiful. You can almost smell it.

Clearly, the times when Mother Mary was speaking were infused with a high spiritual vibration because She was present.

During the times when the Archangels were speaking, I was involved with what I call "transmission channeling." This means that not only were words being channeled but a transmission as well.

A few months *before* the six-week course began, there was an earlier profound evening of transmission channeling and spiritual vision and communication. In the course of preparing this text, it became clear that much of that earlier evening was in fact preparation for the six-week course on the coming of the Cosmic Christ, so it is included as chapter 1 of this book.

A few more important points. First, the communications were given in English, as the audience spoke American English. However, certain terms and phrases were used that were known by those present—most of whom had extensive background in Hinduism, Tibetan Buddhism, Shamanism, and the channeled teachings known as the Michael teachings. These terms and phrases were used by the guides and teachers in order to facilitate our understanding of these sometimes esoteric matters. They are included in a glossary at the back of this book.

Oftentimes, Mother Mary and Archangel Metatron would repeat a phrase. This was for emphasis and for our benefit. Those repetitions were left in. Sometimes, repetitions occurred because I was clarifying what I thought I had just heard. For the most part, redundancies on my part have been deleted from this written text.

Perhaps 98 percent of this written text is directly transcribed from the audio recordings made at the time of the discourses. Editing was kept to an absolute minimum so as to preserve the integrity of the text, even at the expense of "polish." The only liberal editing, done primarily to minimize digressions, occurred in the first chapter when the participants in the circle shared their experiences. Sometimes additional or substitute words or phrases (not in the transcribed text) are included for clarification; these edits are shown in brackets [ ]. (Very minor edits, such as grammatical corrections, are *not* bracketed.)

Because I am an imperfect vessel, certain communications were difficult for me to perceive, and I spoke them awkwardly or tentatively. Any clumsiness or inelegance in the discourses is due to inadequacies in my proper reception of these communications. But even then, I believe the essential transmission is here, and the attentive and open-hearted reader should be able to profit from it.

Oftentimes, Mother Mary and Archangel Metatron would announce themselves. If the text reads, "Mother Mary speaks," Mother Mary is actually saying those words. It is not an editorial device. Each speaker is introduced by a small-caps bold name, such as "**MOTHER MARY:**".

Throughout these communications and transmissions, you will find unending, universal compassion and tolerance. Christ is not the property of any church, sect, or group of believers. Mother Mary is not owned by the Roman Catholic or the Eastern Orthodox churches. Christ and Mother Mary exist far outside the scope of humble humanity and their organizations. No matter what your religious or spiritual preference, I hope this text increases your free heart-awakening to greater love, compassion and tolerance.

Tambor Solana
San Rafael, California
November 1996

CHAPTER ONE

‛The ‛Prophecies

MARCH 7, 1996
MILL VALLEY, CALIFORNIA

*Present: Shelley, Mitchell, Annie, Lance, Fritz, Devaka,
Chris, Karaina, Roxanne, and Solana.*

SOLANA: You all here have been called for a very special reason, and I am talking spiritually here. And a lot of what I am saying I am channeling, and we will talk about it later. But the line that came in [from just a minute ago] was that "you are the first sacrifice"— meaning you are part of the first wave who are embodying a higher vibration. So, conventionally speaking, it is like a sacrificial act, a spiritual act. And the other three [persons] who couldn't make it tonight are just with us in spirit, a step behind, and (this is so Shiva-like, all the Shivaites will love this) their [ego] "death warrants" are signed too. We're talking about Lia, Sephira, and Karla.

There are different masters that are going to come tonight. One is Rudi,[1] Swami Rudrananda, who was the first guru of [the American-born Master] Da Free John [now known as Adi Da], and who was a kundalini Tantric Adept. And he will be speaking. I have never seen him on the subtle plane or channeled him before. I didn't even know [he would be here] until we sat down [just now and] I saw his face talking. There will also probably be more kundalini activation today too, if it is not already happening for you all. [And] Archangel Metatron and Archangel Uriel are here and the Christ is here—*the Christ is here.* And I was told that the seriousness of this is something we don't, [and] I don't understand. Earlier, I was admonished for not taking it seriously enough to have the tape recorder handled. So it is my fault. I apologize for not starting this [session] fifteen minutes earlier and making not only you wait but all our friends on the other side of the veil wait.

Rudi is coming in now. Rudi has a lot of laughter. And Rudi is going to channel a kundalini vibration through my body, through my wrists into Shelley and Mitchell and on to you [in the circle] and on to Devaka. And Devaka, you're exactly opposite me, and so when the energy comes to you I want you to send it back to me through your crown chakra and through your heart chakra. All right—so this is the link-up. And now we can feel this. Different people are going to experience different aspects of the intensification of the kundalini energy in different ways. *[The kundalini vibration gets strongly activated and everyone present goes into a deep meditation for a few minutes.]*

It is going to subside for a little bit. Kundalini vibration is [in the process of] being intensified for everybody. It will affect you in different ways. Watch this in the next few weeks. I want Annie to be able to call Shelley and be in touch with Shelley, not now but in the future. You two have a spiritual support on this kundalini vibration—Mitchell, you with Fritz and Chris; the others with me. It is not that the kundalini isn't always running. It is just that it is being intensified and made more known to you all. Okay?

It will show up in different ways in terms of where the kundalini intensification is moving to release [stuck energy in your body]. If it is active in your second chakra you might cry. You might decide to be celibate for a little while. You might decide to have sex and change your pattern. Anything could happen. If it is in your heart, you might feel sad or go [about] releasing a relationship, or something [else might] happen. If it is in your throat, you might start telling the truth more to somebody. Different things will happen to each individual. **The purpose of this is not to be experiential. The purpose of this is to change you for good.** This is not supposed to be a fun night. This is like taking a part out and putting a new upgrade in. You're getting more "megabytes" in your "computer system."

There are a few other things [for me] to say. I started talking this summer about "the Tree of Life." I am going to remind everybody of this and introduce it to a few people [here] who haven't heard of it. The Tree of Life concept is that everybody has one position on the Tree: root, trunk, limb, branch, twig, leaf. There are different functions. If you're a root person you hold the tree up. You're usually in the earth. You don't move a lot. You don't see the stars much. We depend on you to keep the rent paid, PG&E [the utility bills] paid, the water working, gas in the car. You're not expected to see the blue pearl, all the subtle stuff—you know, angels coming down from heaven. We don't expect you to do that. You're busy holding something else. If all the roots of the tree [see] the stars in heaven, the tree dies. For those [of you] who are root people, do not judge your spiritual experience on [the basis of] visions, sounds, psychic experience. Judge your spiritual experience on [the basis of] love. Do you feel a little more love? Do you feel a little *something*, a little lighter? Annie is a root person. So if Annie feels that, then she is having a massive spiritual experience. We don't expect you to tell us all this other stuff. If you do, that is cool, too.

The other people, who are more [like] branches and limbs, [remember that] everybody has got a function on the tree. There are communicators like Devaka and Roxanne. They're sort of at a place where things branch off into four or five places. So there is a lot of communication going on there. So that is your function —it will be more of a fluid function. Then there are people way out on branches and twigs and leaves, and when the wind blows they flutter all about. They see the stars. They see the birds fly by. And they report all these kinds of things that the trunk and the roots don't see. And when they get too "out there," the trunk and the roots bring them back in.

So we all work together. I want everybody to know that [we] are all are part of the Tree of Life, and the sooner you can find where you are and enjoy that role and honor everybody else's role, then [the sooner] we will really start as a group to be in greater harmony. I don't want people to feel they're not "getting it" for whatever reason. This is very common. Every part of the tree needs the rest of the tree to survive.

Now it is the Christ-Sananda vibration [which] is coming in. *Blessed Be.* I will speak as purely as I can of this vibration, which is a little difficult. Okay, I will repeat. I will speak as best I can of this vibration as I hear it.

†††

CHRIST-SANANDA: Children, your Heavenly Father is eternally blissful and transcendental. You are of that same nature. You have been given free will and individuation to enjoy the kingdom of God. Each of you has a piece of the Divine Father-Mother essence in your heart. But each of you is also a unique character as part of the miracle. Although this is nothing new to you, we want you to feel a sense of the vibration now that is being generated on the higher chakra level to you all. Feel the absolute *peace*. That is it—*the absolute peace*. Remembering your Heavenly Father and Divine Mother is remembering this peace. **You are not separate from God and never will be.** But you are growing in responsibility.

So rejoice and honor that piece of the Divine in everyone else. And what you give to Me from the heart will be returned in kind, purified. So whatever is offered devotionally, purely, will be returned —that peace. And I ask you to pray and you will see that you are never separated or alone.

SOLANA: Sananda is going to step back and Archangel Uriel is coming in now. And Devaka, you can always send that [kundalini] vibration back to me through the heart and seventh chakra.

❖ ❖ ❖

ARCHANGEL URIEL: This is Archangel Uriel. *I am the keeper of all prayers.* All prayers are recorded by the angels. And I am the overseer of every prayer. You imagine that it sounds like a great responsibility—to be responsible for every prayer of all beings, not only in this world, but in other worlds. But we have our version of master computers too.

No prayer goes unheard. Know this. That is all. Archangel Uriel.

SOLANA: Now, Archangel Metatron.

◖ • ◗

ARCHANGEL METATRON: For all those who have been initiated into the Order of the Lamb, we ask you to take the Holy

Object that you've been initiated in. Do not break hands, but take that Holy Object and point the bottom of it up into the center of the circle with your psychic hands and feel the activation of the Archangel of Divine Love.

Behold, for those who are the leaves of the tree, the higher parts of the tree, look and see in the subtle parts of your mind—the Paschal Lamb—the golden sheep, *the golden sheep* that is a symbol of Christ. Agnus Dei [the Lamb of God] is here on the subtle behind us. For those who can see it, it is in gold. You can read in the Book of Revelation about the golden lamb. There will be a few here that will report seeing this—and you can read it in the Book of Revelation.

For some of you I am going to ask—and I am going to start with Annie—I am going to ask you to close your eyes, Annie, and let your attention go above your body. Let your heart relax and let your consciousness go a foot or two above your body, and let the kundalini do its work and let it move in you. That is good. And you can trust that if it goes above your body (that) Solana will be there to make sure you don't leave, or go off to a motel or do something funny! Your consciousness is safe, so you can go very high. Let yourself relax and go high if you want. It will be good for your circuitry, your kundalini circuitry. You can just relax. You will also have two spiritual brothers on either side of you that will keep you safe on the other side. So we want all the women here to feel that they're totally safe. They can really relax. They can cry a little bit if they need to. The energy is very protected. There is a lot of very strong protection, and you can let your guard down spiritually and just receive the benediction, spiritual blessing, the anointing that is present here.

Metatron speaks now. Behold, a great time of purification will come upon the Earth in 1998 and 1999. It is true that the prophecies concerning the southern part of southern California may come to pass. The karmic work that was so well purified in '92 and '93 has met an impasse. The prophecies that had been predicted in '93 and '94, vis-a-vis *Mary's Message to the World*,[2] were allayed because of the prayers of countless people.

But the karmas of masses of people, especially those congregated in southern California, are so strong that they may require this type of catastrophe to remind them that they are part of God and part of God's world.

This must be very clear to you. If anything happens like this it is like a mother reminding a child that they've got a mom and a home. Or else the child will hurt itself. So if such a thing happens it is done under the greatest of mercies. But it is likely, a 70 to 80 percent chance, that there will be major earthquakes in the area between San Diego and Los Angeles in 1998 and 1999 with also activations on the [San] Andreas Fault.

For those of you who are releasing feelings, let your heart also open up to receive the bliss that is coming in. This is good. Whenever there is a release, if there is a replenishment in the heart and in the soul, then the release is permanent. There will also be Earth changes. Earth changes are scheduled in Europe, especially in the northern Portugal and northern Spain area, around 2000-2001, and in other parts of the world: Turkey, Israel, Japan, India, Pakistan, Zaire, Kenya, Uganda, Italy, Greece. These are all scheduled for Earth changes. Some of these vortexes, such as the ones in Greece, are still being used for negative purposes and they need to be cleansed.

I am Archangel Metatron. I am the Shepherd of the shepherds. I am the Lamb and I am the Keeper of the lambs. When you pray to Christ as Shepherd, you pray through me, because there is no difference between the Archangels and the Christ.

At this point Solana will not be in the [San Francisco] Bay Area as of 1998. If the Earth changes continue he will be scheduled to move by that time—by 1998. And there may be some traveling around, including going to places like Idaho and New Mexico and elsewhere. Solana was asked to move in 1993 but the Earth changes were postponed, and a few months before his departure he was told to not move and the Earth changes also did not come to pass. As we know, there were no major earthquakes in the [San Francisco] Bay Area in 1993 even though they were predicted by such folks as Gordon-Michael Scallion and others.[3]

There is more. Again, Solana is channeling this. Do not doubt that you are Christs. And the Christ is also of your nature as well.

Those of you who are all connected to the Order of Melchizedek, you may have connections to other traditions: Shivaite, Native American, Tibetan Buddhist, Umbanda—but you all have a unique connection to the Christ-connection which is being activated at this time. The Christ of the churches is a watered-down version of the purity of the Christ essence. So we also urge you to overcome your past experiences of bad Christianity which is prevalent in your simple society. Even the simple ones get a taste of Christ, but they can only carry the tiniest of the vibration. As you are older, have mercy towards them, be compassionate for even the fundamentalists. Be careful of them because they still can be crazy. But this, *[everyone present in the circle receives an activation of the Christ vibration]* right here, this feeling now, this right here, this is it. Feel this, everybody? There is going to be more now right here. Yes, that—the Lamb and the Lion, that is it.

SANAT KUMAR: Greetings!

SOLANA: This being is laughing at me. Ha, ha, ha, who are you?

SANAT KUMAR: I am Kumar, Sanat Kumar.

SOLANA: He [Sanat Kumar] is sort of saying, he is sort of laughing at Solana, going "Solana is a little new at this, so he gets a little heavy and righteous. He will get better as he gets older, so..." So I am kind of being laughed at. It is okay. I will take it like a man.

SANAT KUMAR: I am Sanat Kumar. Feel my vibration. It is different. I am the lightness of truth. I am the joy of vision. The truth is fun. Do not fear the truth. **So now that you know that the truth is fun, tell the truth.** One of you wrote a play about the truth, and afterwards he can share the story with the group.

Solana had a realization the other day which is actually something that I, Sanat Kumar, gave to him. And it says this:

> *True manhood, true womanhood,*
> *is not being strong, macho, independent.*
> *True manhood or true womanhood*
> *is aligning oneself with the truth.*
> *And it is the truth which is strong.*

Some think that they have to be a man, prove their manhood. But they're being untruthful in reality—meaning they are following an action which is untrue. Such as, "I will rob a bank to prove my manhood." This is not truth. The greatest heroes of your world have been adherents to the truth.

You will find that truth is like layers of an onion. One truth may lead to a deeper truth. So, I am Sanat Kumar. I am the advocate of truth tonight. That is all. Thank you for not watching TV tonight and listening to me.

SOLANA: Okay. Let's break hands. This brings to a conclusion the guest speakers. I think I am going to ask everybody to get back in their bodies, and we will take a minute or two just to stand and stretch. And then we will circle up and talk a little bit about this [evening].

[A few minutes later:] So, I guess now it will be open mike or questions. And what I am mostly interested in is not so much what has been happening in the last few days, unless it particularly related to tonight—if anybody had something that happened in the last few days that they felt particularly related to this evening. Does anybody else want to say anything?

SHELLEY: I do. I first want to give great thanks to Solana for calling me, for having everyone come together for this. I've been feeling the pull for about a week in meditation that the time is at hand for the coming of the Cosmic Christ and that that initiation was going to be coming. And it has terrified me and scared me, and it is was the absolutely one thing that I wanted and prayed for most. So you can imagine the attraction and repelling at the same time that was going on for me. I was getting symbols of crosses and all sorts of things. I was told tonight that the Cosmic Christ would be coming through. The reason I brought the new blossoms [of flowers for the meditation circle tonight is because] this message was given to me right before I left, and it says, "The key note is to open yourselves and consider the significance of this beautiful saying, 'And the day came when the risk to remain tight in a bud was more painful than the risk it took to blossom.'" Praise be to God.

ANNIE: I am very happy to be here, and I am very moved by this initiation ceremony channeling event. I was happy that you called on me in particular to just acknowledge me—*me*—and being in my body and just even further accepting who I am, because it has been so liberating to discover more about me. And that it is quite fun to be a "root," thank you. And it is a metaphor—I do see the stars and I do see the sun and the heavens. So it is really beautiful to feel okay about [being a "root person"]. The Christ-Consciousness has been prevailing with me all my life and it goes in and out; it [has] just been pretty steady recently. So everything you said was pretty much on the mark for me in the last couple weeks. And also [what you said about] living in truth and honoring and being dedicated to truth, especially with my [fiancé] Mike. And we do need to remember that we are Gods, and that God is within us at all times. And so it was a nice reminder.

LANCE: I have avoided circles like this for a while. I haven't felt like this in years and I've always had a lot of apprehension and anxiety around change—not just for me but for the world and for the planet and for everyone. I [have often gotten] fed up and incredibly impatient, [and] I've been waiting a long time for things to change. [And] this is the first time in a while that I have really felt like things can start moving again. I am grateful for being back here. And I hope that I get to make a movie about lying. I wrote a screenplay the first year I was in Hollywood, which was about four years ago when I was idealistic and thought I could change the world. And it was about—well, I come from a very mendacious background. I grew up believing that lying was the only and true form of communication—that manipulation was the right way to get what you want—a very Machiavellian perspective and pretty negative, but I had no idea. [Then] I got into college and I understood and realized that there was a different way of living. And now [even though I] have kind of gone the other way [toward being brutally honest], I still unfortunately am addicted to lying. So I hear myself lying sometimes, and have to laugh at that also.

I wrote a script about these stockbrokers who were both liars, and one of them got caught lying and was fired. And his friend and he were sitting at the bar after he got fired, and his friend said to him, "Well, you know you got fired because you're just a bad liar." And [he says] "What are you talking about? I don't lie. Everybody does what I do!" [His friend responds,] "No, they don't. We do this to get where we want. And nobody else lies like you lie. You're like Super Liar." So he gets caught and he gets fired. And he comes to the realization, "Oh, My God, I do, I lie all the time." And his friend gives him all these examples of how he lied just in the last fifteen minutes. So he and his friend make a bet to see who can stop lying the longest. His friend, a kind of John Belushi, only lasts about a week. He tells some girl he's a doctor or something so he can get her in bed. And his friend, the protagonist in the story, never lies again. Obviously no one is perfect, but he basically completely and totally changes his life.

I am very excited to be here and I am grateful that you called me. Thank you everyone, really.

FRITZ: I feel very grateful, and this is wonderful. And I am scared. It has been really intense for days. So I am glad it came to culmination. I enjoyed especially the last one [Sanat Kumar] that was so incredibly blissful. One of my spiritual names is Kumara and I never could make sense of this name. Years ago I was given this name by a guru. And so now I know! And for a while [tonight] I had this kind of split where part of me was really enjoying it and then another part—[my internal critic]—

I am not sure how to explain it, but I don't believe in God as a super-daddy or super-mommy kind of thing. So, I have this [internal] critic going, you know, feeling patronized, and *somebody's there playing father and calling me child. [Lots of laughter.]* I do not like that at all. And even if it is *God* I don't like it, you know. *[More laughter.]* But I go with it.

SOLANA: I want you to know that when I heard it—I am like, what? Children? You want me to say "children" to this group of friends? *[More laughter.]* Yes, I was negotiating [with the Masters].

FRITZ: But I understand also that they, the beings, are behaving in some archetypal [way]—they have kind of an archetypal function. And so most of me doesn't have to explain everything. So I guess that is part of my purification. So the critic [in me] can become a little bit smaller. And I am very grateful. I feel wonderful. I feel more myself right now. Thanks.

MITCHELL: Well, I guess in the same way that Fritz liked the Sanat Kumara vibration, I felt that the Metatron [communication] was the most important and the most powerful—for a few reasons, one [of which is] the love aspect. You know, I feel that that is the most lasting thing. Whether one exists or doesn't exist, *the love is the most important thing.* Whether one is in this world or not in this world. And I felt that the feeling of Metatron as being the Shepherd was very important because I felt that he's the one that guards the chelas, the disciples.

SOLANA: *Chelas* is a Hindu word for students or devotees.

MITCHELL: Yes, in the same way that in the Hindu tradition the Lord of the world, Krishna, has Shiva, who is the guru who takes care of the souls in the intermediary [states], but at the same time is one with the Lord and not different. In the same way Metatron—it seems that he's the one that guards the chelas and helps them, you know. And I felt the love aspect involved with that. [That] particular kind of love seems to me to be very, very important.

SOLANA: Did anyone get a sense of the Lamb that I talked about?

OTHERS: Yes. I felt it. Yeah.

MITCHELL: Yes, I saw that Lamb.

SOLANA: For those who did, please read the Book of Revelation.

MITCHELL: I did experience the Lamb, a golden Lamb. I feel that the vibration of Metatron is something that is able to really rescue people. I feel that that is what we are talking about here, about people's responsibility and all of this. And so it seems to me very important to keep the connection and link with this particular vibration.

CHAPTER TWO

The Feminine Side of the Christ

MAY 7, 1996
SAN RAFAEL, CALIFORNIA

Present: Devaka, Howard, Lia, Shelley, Chris, and Solana.

SOLANA: Tonight we're called to listen to the message of Mary and whatever other teachers and Masters want to come. Tonight's topic is going to be the coming of the Cosmic Christ.

✿

*M*OTHER MARY: First of all, southeastern Europe is in disarray, and there are great calamities that are happening in the former Republic of Yugoslavia. And Mother Mary has been working very hard to minimize human suffering there, but the forces of negativity and karma are very great there. This is a thorn in the side of the Holy Mother, and She is watching this circumstance night and day like a concerned mother whose children are sick and possibly dying. And She is nursing them and tending to them, and they're intent on killing one another. And the grief that is being created from this is something only the Divine Christ Father Vibration can neutralize because of its collective weight.

Your Mother has many forms—Quan Yin, Tara, Kali, Saraswati [to name a few]—but here in the West, the form that is known to most of you is Mary, Mother of Jesus. Truly, all these faces of the Mother are attributes of the One, Divine Power which is neither male nor female, but is nevertheless God. This is a profound mystery, and even though in principle it is simple, in practice it is reserved for the wise. So God shows Himself/Herself in many forms so that the fragments of Divine Consciousness can realign themselves to the Great Liberating Process of Truth with forms that will not overwhelm the sense of individuality.

So, My children, take heart. God will reach you in many ways and with many voices over time.

And now I have messages for some of you. The first message is for Chris. Chris, you should consider bankruptcy[4] or getting help with your financial circumstance. You have carried much financial weight and we ask you to ask for professional help with this. This is important for you to look at. You have a great spiritual birthright and we want you to be able to enjoy your spirituality in the course of your career preparation. And angels will be sent to you to help you find ways to have more levity and fun during this time. And we ask you to talk to Solana about some of these matters because he is a spiritual brother for you. And we wish you to receive this as much as you can, because we want you to enjoy your spirituality now and let your career not be your primary focus. It might be a very, very important focus, but not what runs your life. And it is weighing you down, and we want you to be happy.

There is a message for Howard. Howard, your financial circumstance will be changing within six months for the better. We're not exactly sure the karma with Raylene and John that Solana was talking about is the right one for you. But there will be [good] things coming your way and we want you to know that will be happening, that you will find more of the right livelihood that you are looking for.

Shelley, we want to talk to you about your son, Nicolas. There was a correct noticing [by you] about your son's Tibetan lifetimes. Your son has been a high Tibetan lama—we're feeling [that he was] of the Gelukpa tradition. And you might want to have some of the Tibetan artifacts around him to see how he responds to them. And when some of the lamas come, perhaps you could see if it is right to take him to see them. Relative to your partner and husband, we are feeling that he is resisting, but [that] he will within eight months—we don't want to use the word "cave in"—but within eight months [he] will understand things in a new light.

Devaka, we feel that the partnering that you are looking for may come, but you have a real need to not only purify karmas at this time but to lay a very extensive network, a groundwork of healing and examination and exploration, so that you can become a very effective counselor and teacher—and that this will really begin to manifest in the next decade. If you found the true partner now, on an essence level you would feel that you didn't really examine everything that you wanted to in order to become as experienced a teacher and counselor as you would like to. This is something we are feeling on an essence level. And so understand that your Divine Parents, your Higher Essence, will steer you towards the right partnering when your coursework is done. And this is a course that is an independent study, so called, that you've set up yourself on a higher level. Okay? This partnering might not occur for 24 to 36 months, which might seem like a long time, but some of the things that you have lined up for yourself in the next period of time will be so valuable for you that you will see this. Now, this is not set in stone, but this is an 80 percent probability at this time.

Lia, we have a message for you which is about your daughter. We wish that you pray to Mother Mary and the angels for your daughter. And it is not that your daughter is in danger or there is anything difficult. It is that your daughter identifies with her father's emotionality, and by praying to us you will be able to help her individuate more and understand her own stuff more. Does this make sense to you? This may be something you are aware of or that you are not aware of. Some of these dynamics are subtle and some are not so subtle. We ask that you not do anything more than you are doing already on a personal level, but we do ask that you pray to the Divine Mother, the Divine Feminine, on behalf of your daughter, so that she has more individuation and can understand when her emotions are her own versus when she's been empathetic with her father. This is not something that you have to do for a long time. It might be something you do weekly for a period of three or four months. Does that make sense? This is a gift for you and it will be a beneficial scene for you and your family.

We wish everybody now to uncrunch their shoulders. Now how does one uncrunch their shoulders? First, sit up a little straighter, and second, as you inhale let the air not only fill your belly but fill the upper part of your lungs, and as the air rises up the muscles in the shoulder will relax. Uncrunch if you will. And as you do this, keep your head a little straight, your spine a little straight, and let the muscles relax. You will find some extra energy being generated, especially some mental energy, so that you will be able to have more alertness for the rest of our communication.

Children, this is a world of polarity. When there is dark, there is light. When there is evil, there is good. When there is the most good, there is the most evil. The life of Jesus is an example of the most good partnering up with the most evil. During wars there is evil and good. Bosnia is an example of evil and good, played out on a more grand global level with players from not only this world but from other universes coming in to create karma or to purify karma.

One of the gifts that I as Mary show you is the feminine side of the Christ. In the higher dimensional planes there is no anthropomorphic difference between the aspects of Divine Personalities. There is not a separate little [Saint] Peter and apostles, and on the higher levels there is not a separate Mary or Christ or even the Archangel Michael vibration—although on this [physical] level it seems like [there are], and they are presented as somewhat fragmented. But Mary, I as Mary, am showing you the feminine aspect of what the Christ vibration is. And we are going to activate that for everybody now, so that they can sense this in their own souls, hearts and selves. And this can also be for anybody else listening, because the cassette tape will be vibrated with this code.

We ask you to visualize a lamb in your heart, *Agnus Dei*, the Divine Lamb.

If you can see it, that is good. If you cannot see it, either visualize that you can or hold the feeling of that tenderness of a very young lamb. To Mary, all of God's creation looks like a lamb. All beings are precious and beloved such as the lamb that you visualize in your heart. If you hold [this vision] with the most tender preciousness, then [you can feel the] covering, the sweetness of protecting creation. In some ways Mother Mary's vibration is a cover, a covering. In the prayer

> *"Hail Mary, full of Grace,*
> *[the Lord is with Thee,]*
> *blessed art Thou amongst all women,*
> *and blessed is the fruit of thy womb"*

"blessed is the fruit of thy womb" refers to that covering, and *"blessed"* is the lamb within your heart.

Within your own heart, you could say that your own heart is a womb for the Divine child within you. So, you cover—like your beloved baby, you cover that with a blanket to keep it warm and safe. As you learn to do this within your own heart, you will [then] be able to do it with the whole world, the whole cosmos. But first we begin with ourselves. So an esoteric understanding of *"blessed is the fruit of thy womb"* refers to you. "The *fruit* of thy womb" refers to the Christ, the precious part of the Christ-lamb within your own heart which is thy womb. Do you understand this?

Are there any questions at this time, anybody here? Lia, do you have a question? Anybody?

CHRIS: Yes, I have a question.

MOTHER MARY: Yes, Chris.

CHRIS: You said I should put my work off, as sort of like a part of my life and not like my main focus. I wonder if you could elaborate on that some more.

MOTHER MARY: Yes, Chris, we want you to look in the mirror sometime. When you look in the mirror you will see Chris. You will see you, essentially in that moment free and happy. One of the things you choose to do is to build a career. It should always be secondary to your happiness as an individual. In order to do that there will need to be a stronger sense of self. If you perhaps choose to do this practice just described, [the practice] of the Lamb within your own heart, that might lead you more into the state we are talking about. There are many practices that can. This is one of them. You are forgetting yourself somewhat and thus you're getting ensnared a little and you are not joyful like we know your nature is. It is almost like you are doing work as penance, or work has become penance for you. And this is one orientation you can have, but not the one we wish you to have. It is not necessary from our point of view. So, Chris, if you will open in this moment right here, we are going to help you feel something that will help this process we are talking about.

[Chris receives a vibration of spiritual energy in his heart.]

That is a start. Let **JOY** be the answer instead of reasons or words. Does this make sense?

CHRIS: Yes.

MOTHER MARY: JOY in and of itself has a momentum that can embrace and transmute into itself. But let **JOY** be the answer, versus the mind, reasons and concepts.

CHRIS: Thank you.

MOTHER MARY: Of course.

SOLANA: Now, we are going to talk about the coming of the Cosmic Christ. Mary is going to step aside for awhile. And Archangel Lord Metatron [will come], the Messenger of the Lamb himself. You will feel a change in the vibrational frequency coming in now.

◗ • ◗

ARCHANGEL METATRON: Lord Metatron says, *feel me* in the heart. Feel me. I am a rare presence. Certainly I am a Master of the second chakra and the sixth chakra as Solana has described earlier [in other gatherings]. But primarily I am a vibration in the heart—a kind of samadhi. Please fall into this feeling now if you can. Good.

I am Metatron. I am an expression of the Christ, of the Christos. I am the Sign of the Shepherd and of what is shepherded. I am the Shepherd's Staff. I am the One who gathers all the lost children of the universe back into the path of righteousness.

Yes, the time of the Cosmic Christ is coming. In Earth time it may manifest more in the years 2030 and 2040, as it is likely that an Infinite Soul[5] will appear in the years from 2017 to 2023. There are several candidates being prepared for this, high souls who are finishing their final life cycles on Earth, who have volunteered for the hazardous and enlightened task of carrying the Infinite Soul vibration. Among these are a Mayan woman from Central America, who is a young girl now, who has been training for this for many lifetimes. There are also others scattered around the world.

Yes, the Christ vibration will be known again but it will be known in a unified way—in a greater, more unified way of Divine Female and Divine Male. Look at your hands—there is left and right. They form the prayer sign at the heart. This is a riddle.

[Note—at this point a portion of the transmission is missing from the tape. The following is a reconstruction of this section:] Hold your left hand up at heart level, and hold your right hand up at heart level. Turn them so they face one another. Slowly bring them towards one another, like two lovers slowly walking towards one another. The hands represent female and male, left and right, equally attracted, reflections of each other. In your left hand, you can feel the pressure of the energy between your hands. [At this point the recording resumes:] And in your right hand, as you put them closer together, you can feel the pressure between your hands. They touch, they unite at the heart. Left and right. Male and female. At the heart. Thank you. You can put your hands down if you like.

This has not been the theology of the last few thousand years of the main sects that have taught what the brother Sananda-Christ, Lord Jesus taught. Lord Jesus did not teach the left hand or the right hand. He taught both hands, uniting with the Father through the Morning Star, which is an esoteric portal to the higher realms. Yes, it is true that Christ was a great Yogi and in secret He taught and prepared initiates when He could find them. Nicodemus was such an initiate, as were a few of the Apostles. But in general, He found ordinary people who needed to be taught love in ordinary, living terms.

I have spoken the prophecy of the Infinite Souls. You can make notes of that, and there will be further clarification of this by the one who will speak after me. I, as Metatron, thank you for feeling and being with me this evening. And now I will leave.

SOLANA: Archangel Gabriel is coming next.

* * *

ARCHANGEL GABRIEL: The Trumpet of Gabriel is being warmed up, but it is not sounded yet. Look for the years 2008 through 2012. This does tie in to the twenty-year cycle that Solara talked about in the 11:11[6] from 1992 to 2012. Although some of her information is not exact, her general outline of this twenty-year cycle has much validity to it. But, on a more personal matter, the Trumpet of Gabriel also refers to esoteric sounds within the body, the kundalini, what some [spiritual] paths call the *shabd*—the inner sounds, the higher sounds, the high-pitched sounds that one hears sometimes, the Flute of Krishna—which also aligns one to God. These are within the *orchestra* of Gabriel, Gabriel's Trumpet. They are not different in principle. So, Gabriel's Trumpet not only is an external affair but is an individual affair. So, if and when you hear these internal sounds, the high-pitched frequency-alignments, they are also calling you to an incoming or descent of the Divine in your own body-mind.

SOLANA: Archangel Gabriel is now leaving and Mary will be returning.

MOTHER MARY: Children, My Son Jesus died to advance humanity on its next step of evolution. He was an archetype and an epitome of the Sacrifice that was required to bring humanity up. In the

Michael Teaching, it was acknowledged that Christ's Sacrifice, the Sacrifice of the Infinite Soul, Who Jesus lived as for the last short period of His life, changed the color of the Earth's society from a Baby Soul population to a Young Soul population. His was the final coin which was a profound payment and sacrifice on this level.

The Young Soul cycle, which has been extant for the last two thousand years, has been one of *teenagerism*. Look at your own teenagers, look at you as a teenager. What do teenagers do? They grow up, they make mistakes, they drink [alcohol], they stay up until all hours. They're not children, they're certainly not adults. The last two thousand years has been a teenagerism. The next millennium or two will be [a period] transitioning out of the teenagerism for a significant part of the souls that inhabit the world/Gaia/Earth at this time. Many teenagers drive their parents mad or numb during their time of being teenagers. It has been a difficult time for the Divine, the Parents, so to speak. If you use this as a metaphor you will understand what we are saying. But we think it is a good metaphor that you all can understand. It is important to understand this.

The coming of the Cosmic Christ is about new teachings of Christ—superior teachings. What do teenagers understand? They understand curfews at 11:00 PM. Do not do LSD in the ninth grade. They understand simple things. They will still push and bend and try to break those things as well. Likewise, much of the common teachings affiliated with Christ are teachings for children and teenagers. Many of us have understood that, and that is why at an earlier age we abandoned them, because even if we were eight or ten or twelve [years old] we knew at a soul level that we were not little children or teenagers, that we needed teachings more suitable to our soul age. So we abandoned [traditional] Christianity en masse, especially for the teachings of the East—Tibet, Thailand, Burma, India—which address teachings for older humans, older than fourteen, twelve and nine [years old].

The teachings of the Cosmic Christ are about teachings for older people. Just as a teenager, who is thirteen or fourteen, cannot be expected to be married or have a healthy [sexual] relationship, likewise the teachings of the Unified Christ-Consciousness are about a Divine Marriage of the feminine and masculine attributes of Christ and can only be expected of older people. Just as you would not talk to a twelve-year-old about marriage, but you could talk to a twenty-five-year-old about marriage. Do you understand this? Therefore, we cannot expect the teenagers or children to understand the Unified Christ-Consciousness teaching because they still need to individuate, just like a teenager does. To simply know about Mary or Christ is appropriate, as simply to know about being a girl or a boy is appropriate for a teenager. However, there are enough souls on the Earth at this time who are ready for a higher, unified teaching.

This teaching will come and it will be brought with a great force. There are purges that are scheduled for the planet. There are pockets of suffering and stagnation and stultification that need to and will be purified. Some of these have to do with the consciousness that pervades the space. We think it was the philosopher Teilhard de Chardin who talked about a sphere of consciousness that pervades the mind-set.

SOLANA: He might have used the word ionosphere, I forget— you can help us if anybody knows.

DEVAKA: Noösphere.

MOTHER MARY: Noösphere. There are pockets of the noösphere that are blemished or turned in on themselves that need to be realigned for the health of the entire population and for Mother Earth Herself. So, these purges are planned just like one might plan to go to the dentist [or dermatologist] in a month to have a tooth removed or to have a blemish removed. Likewise, there are trips planned to the dentist and dermatologist on Earth in the next twenty years. During this time there will appear to be great calamities and sudden losses, all of which are administered on a higher level, according to great, meticulous care and precision, taking into account the laws of karma and retribution, of individual choice and group and soul family choice. Be prepared for these, for the news, and know that it is a shrugging off of the old and a reinvigoration for the whole. It is within the context of these changes that there will be more receptivity to the teachings of the Cosmic Christ, for they go against much of what has been taught in earlier Christianity.

First, remember that you are both male and female. The women carry more female vibration and will always be more suited to carry the female essence but will always have some male vibration, and vice versa for the men. Learn to honor the male and female within oneself and how they align with the *Christos*, which is not only a Divine Attribute of existence but is also encoded within your own heart chakra.

This is all for tonight. There will be more discourse and sharing in the next several weeks. The most important thing we wish to say to you is, remember tonight's feelings. Remember the feelings, the transmissions that were shared. This is what theology forgets. **Theology loves to remember the words and loves to forget the feeling.** Let us not be theologians. Let us be rememberers, devotees of the feeling. That is all from Mary; good night.

CHAPTER THREE

The Bounty in Your Hands
MAY 14, 1996
SAN RAFAEL, CALIFORNIA

Present: Solana, Lia, Shelley, and Howard.

SOLANA: We will say the Rosary three times. If you know it, join in please.

Hail Mary, full of Grace,
The Lord is with thee.
Blessed art thou amongst all women,
And blessed is the fruit of thy womb, Jesus.

Holy Mary, Mother of God,
Pray for us now, and forevermore.
Amen.
      [Repeated two more times]

❦

MOTHER MARY: Mother Mary speaks. Greetings. I've come because you have created a space for Me to come. Likewise, I come into your body when you have created a space in your body for Me to come into. The same is true for My Son and the Holy Father. Thus, do spiritual practice. Make a space for the Trinity. Yes, I said the Trinity, because Mother Mary is part of the Trinity, the Holy Spirit, the Goddess Power. Make a space in the body and then We will come. Likewise, make a space in your home, and We will come too. Make a space in your mind and We will speak through your mind. For We are the Divine Trinity of Christed-Love that is your very nature. Mother Mary speaks. The little Lambs in your heart, did you see them this week? Did you call to them? Did you cover them? They are your inner nature. They are the ones that wish to be recognized. So tend to your flock first. It is easier to tend to the flock in your heart, and then you can tend to the flock that you have karmas with, to teach and to help. So be a good shepherd to yourself and then you can shepherd others. This is also the teaching of Archangel Metatron. But the Lamb in your heart, let it be revealed to you. Say My prayer. Say the Rosary. And let the Lamb be revealed to you. And then the deepest self-love will grow in yourself, and this will make you peaceful and strong and a bastion of strength for all the others who have lost the Lamb in their own hearts.

Mother Mary speaks. Yes, a man can speak My words. Thus Solana speaks My words. Listen, for he has let part of his mind be open through prayer and preparation so that Mother Mary may speak. Your world is filled with insanity. Look at the newspapers. Every day this insanity is reported. New wars, new bombings, new murders, new assassinations. But yet the masses remain unmoved, deadened. I shake My head in Mother's Love. What will it take for My children to pray? How many more horrors do they need to read about to see the state of the world? For all you listening, cannot you spare even half an hour a week to pray for your fellow man? Why not sit in groups around the world and pray for your fellow man? This will create a vibratory wavelength that will ease much suffering. There is a gift in prayer as well. It is the gift of self-forgetting and of identification with compassion. That is a great gift with a very small price to pay.

Mother Mary speaks. The political situation in southeastern Europe may get worse. It is possible that the area known as Macedonia and northeastern Albania and the area where the Kosovo—we believe this is correct—the Kosovo Albanians could get drawn into further political and ethnic strife. These possible scenarios are for 1998—late 1998 and 1999. The people in this region who wear My Son's cross and fight their neighbors mock His name and spit on His memory. They take themselves out of the sphere of blessing and heap karmic retribution upon themselves. This is a good area of the world to pray for. When My servant Solana goes there, near there, in June of 1996, there will be instructions that he will have to help realign the magnetic grid near the city of Szeged in southeastern Hungary that ties in. We will talk a little about this magnetic grid work, and at this point, the tape is to be turned off [as Solana receives specific instructions].

[A few minutes later:]

Mother Mary speaks. If you look at a globe you will see that there are grid lines up and down. Yes, the Earth is a magnetic force-field. It has force-fields [grid lines] that pervade it, perpendicular and vertical and horizontal to the force-fields. These lines can be purified and helped with prayer. If you will look at the grid lines, you will see that some of the grid lines intersect or come near to many of the difficult places in the planet today. One of the grid lines, a few years ago, was the grid line that pervaded Ethiopia. It also went through Kampuchea, or Cambodia, as well as other difficult spots on the Earth where there is suffering. There are other grid lines that affect other political spots too. So you can look at the globe and learn how some of these things work, and in your prayer you can also pray for the grid lines. We are going to teach forms of praying for the grid lines now.

As you pray, you can say "In the Name of the Father, and of the Son, and of the Holy Spirit."

When you say, "In the Name of the Father," imagine the Father-Vibration above the north pole.

[When you say] "of the Son," [imagine the Son-Vibration] below the south pole.

[When you say] "of the Holy Spirit," [imagine the] energy that pervades the world itself. So, "In the Name of the Father, [and of] the Son, and of the Holy Spirit"—this is a blessing of the entire world and it also has to do [with the revelation that through prayer the] *Father descends.*

The Son is the manifestation or the sacrifice of the Father. So the Son is at the south. Do you understand this?

And the Earth pervades—is [pervaded by] the Goddess Power.

So you can pray "In the Name of the Father, [and of] the Son, and [of] the Holy Ghost [Holy Spirit]." And in the center of Gaia, Mother Earth, is a heart—*is a heart*. And you can pray that that heart of the Mother Earth be vibrated with purple and silver as a color of bliss. *Purple* and *silver* are good colors now for the process that Mother Earth is going through.

In the Name of the Father, and of the Son,
and of the Holy Spirit
May the central heart of Mother Earth be pervaded
With the bliss that has the vibration
of purple and silver.

You can end the prayer with "Da"[7] if you want to. "Da, may that be true for the Mother Earth."

Yes, the angels, the angelic beings, help feed Mother Earth through prayer. They feed Her and She feeds all Her creatures and Her children. Imagine—it is a beautiful cycle of giving and receiving on many levels of being.

The gridwork—there are certain gridworks that are not to be touched because the vibrations are very difficult. When you begin to pray for the grids, we ask that you do not be cowboys and go to the worst spots on the grid unless you are asked to do so by a great intuition. Just as you don't clean out the fireplace without gloves or your hands will get very dirty, likewise certain gloves are needed before certain grids are worked on. But you can pray for the grids. Even pray for the equator. You can see the equator is wobbling a little. The equator wobbles just a little bit because the Earth is going through a transformation. If you look at the globe as if you can see North America and South America, the equator to the left of that area is wobbling down a little bit. It is not a precursor for a magnetic pole-shift, but is a precursor of the transmutation that is affecting the globe itself, you see.

There may be repercussions of this equator shift. Earthquakes are an example of this. You can pray for the equator, that it become stable and peaceful, but it is also true that the Earth is being raised up to a higher vibration. And part of the secrets of the 11.11, the twenty-year period, is that by the year 2012 the equator will be in this new position—of a higher vibration, of a higher intensity.

Let's say the equator has been vibrating at a certain level and now it starts to—it is going to go from "55 mph" to "60 mph." As it starts to speed up to 56 and 57, the rest of the equator doesn't quite [immediately follow]—it is not a secure movement. The rest of the world—the equator pervades the world, and the rest of the Earth is catching up to speed, and it is adjusting, and it is going to pick up speed slowly and evenly over this next sixteen years and then it will emerge in this new vibration. And this vibration is the one which will welcome the Infinite Soul or Souls, because there may be two or three that come after the 2012 period.

Mother Mary speaks. For those of you who wish to pray for Mother Earth, this prayer we have described is a beautiful and useful prayer. You may also pray that the Earth is blessed with green—that the exterior of the Earth is blessed with a green vibration, a healthy green vibration at the outside of the Earth. Green is the color of the heart, it is the color of the vitality [of life], it is the color of chi. As you bless the Earth this way you also will feel this green and this chi in your own body-mind. And it will freely move to the places in your own body-mind that need to be harmonized with this [vibration]. You will find that if you pray for your Mother Earth, then your life will take on a new synchronicity. It will become more sensitive to the rhythms of the Earth and the gifts of the Earth, including Nature and the animals, and the devas that are here.

Mother Mary speaks. Children, I rest in a Transcendental Cosmic Samadhi. And the Earth is one of the precious gems that I guard over inside and out. I am always available to prayer, and I have many gifts for those who call upon Me. I will now take My leave for a time, as one of the Archangels will speak soon. Praise be to God and All that Is.

SOLANA: It is Archangel Gabriel who comes with his Trumpet, his Joymaker. He says—

* * *

ARCHANGEL GABRIEL: Yes, Shelley, did you like my sound that stimulated you today? And Lia, you will hear my sound more too, as all of you will. As Gabriel, I always announce the Ever-Free, Ever-Realized, Ever-Already-Perfect State of the Divine Father-Mother God. I announce this in all places and times—the Ever-Perfect Condition.

So when it is said, "Prepare ye the Way of the Lord," that is a paradox, because the Way of the Lord has already happened, the Way of the Lord has already arrived. It is just that we must see it, and through time and space that looks like a preparation.

So, prepare ye the Way of the Lord. I am Gabriel. I bid you well. I bid you peace. I will come again. And soon Metatron will speak. Feel the different vibration that comes.

◄ • ►

ARCHANGEL METATRON: Hallelujah, Praise to God in the Highest! This is Metatron, Servant, Enjoyer of the *Christos*. Throughout all the world, throughout the cosmos, the galactic enjoyment, the Divine Father is blessing the Earth these days. Hold your hands up in prayer and receive the golden drops that come from the Highest Throne Rooms of the God-Worlds. In a wink of an eye, the Divine Father can change the destinies of countless millions of beings. And at this time the Grace of the Divine Father-Mother God is coming. It has come and it is coming.

So, make yourself wealthy with Spirit. Let the gold make you spiritually rich, rich in gold. You can rub this gold all over your body like a shiny gold coin. And store the treasure in your heart. Then you will not be afraid of death, of yourself or those you love.

So we ask you to open your hands in a cupped position. A prayer will be said on your behalf:

Holy Father, Divine Mother
I am an emanation of You.
I live in You as You live in me.
May Your Bounty transform my life in waves of joy.
Amen.

And you can feel the bounty in your hands and you can take the bounty and put it in your heart. And then when you meet poor people who have no gold in their heart you can bless them. You can give them a golden coin or two because you can always go to the Bank of Prayer. And if they refuse the coin and they throw it away, don't worry. It is shiny. Someone else will come and pick it up. So the gift is not a waste. So this is spiritual economics. And your Divine Father-Mother, not like the U.S. Treasury, is the Source of endless Gold, not paper.

I have spoken. This is Archangel Metatron. That is my message for you tonight.

CHAPTER FOUR

The Clarion Call

MAY 21, 1996
MILL VALLEY, CALIFORNIA

Present: Lia, Howard, Mitchell, Roxanne,
Fritz, Shelley, and Solana.

SOLANA: These teachings are being given by Lord Mary, Mother Mary. And we will begin tonight with saying the rosary six times. So for those who want to join in, please do.

Hail Mary, full of Grace,
the Lord is with thee.
Blessed art thou amongst all women,
And blessed is the fruit of thy womb, Jesus.

Holy Mary, Mother of God,
Pray for us now, and forevermore.
Amen.
[Repeated five more times]

❀

*M*OTHER MARY: Good evening. I welcome all My children and those who love Christ who have come tonight to listen. Tonight there will be important teachings that will be shared with all. There will also be inner teachings shared with all. So please breathe deep, relax, open your mind. Receive the distribution of the spiritual treasures that will be given tonight.

Last week we talked about the gridwork that was being worked on. Tonight we wish to elaborate on this. The grid structure was set up eons ago to create a force field for the beauty of nature to evolve in a free, but also a controlled way—to experiment with climate, with life forms. This has been a Divine experiment that has been moved through for a few billion years. Some of you were involved in some of the construction of the gridwork before the planet was created. And some of you in the circle were present, and some of you remember this.

The creation of the Earth was a joyous occasion. So, in the birthing of human/Divine consciousness on Earth which occurred really a few million years ago, the processing and transmutation of the human consciousness has been a—to describe it as a Divine process does not do it justice. It can only be described as a process that God, the Divine Person, Himself/Herself undergoes.

It is almost—to put it in humorous human terms, imagine that God goes to a clothing store and tries on many different outfits. And some of the outfits are beautiful. And maybe He'll wear a polka-dotted sports coat. And maybe He'll come in wearing all black leather. And God tries on all these different clothes. And for God to walk in and try an outfit on and leave, might be a hundred thousand years of your time. Does this make sense? And looking for the right outfit but being willing to experiment on all levels. From the Divine point of view, God's point of view, it is like that, but in human terms it is a hundred thousand years of history.

Now there is a time that is occurring in the planet in which God wants to try on a nicer looking shirt. He's gone through a [period], [has] just worn an outfit that [He now] wants to change. And so, as this new outfit is being put on, there are transformations that are going on that is are shaking everybody up. As if each of you is a molecule in the shirt or the coat that God is wearing. And when the coat is taken off you feel something.

So how does this affect you individually? The important thing that you must know, as we stated last time in one of the prayers we gave you, is that

> **God is in you and you are in God.**
> **This is the highest understanding**
> **that an incarnated personality can have.**

You are in God and God is in you—because of the paradoxical nature of individuated consciousness being part of Divine consciousness. So, if you learn this, and are willing to teach yourself, remind yourself of this: A paradox means two contradictory things occurring simultaneously. The fact that there can be an individuated consciousness within a Divine consciousness is a paradox. So if you remind yourself of both sides of the paradox, then you will understand.

So, as you're settled in this circumstance of working with the paradox, then how you are moved and where you are moved will be of less concern to you. In truth your form, your physical form, is also like a garment. You are also beings that wear many clothes. To put it very simply, it is like on a great, great level, your body is like a sock. One day you wear your blue socks and at the end of the day you take your blue socks off, or you take your blue sock off and you throw it in the hamper. From the Divine Consciousness part that is you, that is what this body is like. And so, some day this form of you will be thrown in the hamper, because it is of no longer any use. But meanwhile, now that it has use for you, let's talk about ways that you can be aligned with the changes that are happening.

We ask you to remember to pray. And in praying you will connect with your higher intuition and with the God-Source. And that will give you your response to what your day or life is supposed to be. So please pray, please open and please listen. Recently someone said, "Yes, I pray all the time," and the response to this person was, "Yes, but you never listen!" And so the answers to prayer are often very subtle and very given. And so, *listen*. Once the prayer is made, listen. If you look at the books on Milarepa, the great Tibetan yogi, he is shown with his hand cupped over his ear. This is a great symbol. Here is a great yogi and what is his symbol? He is the patron saint of Tibet. His symbol is that he is *listening*. He is open to Divine information and intuition. So, please listen once you've made the prayer.

Some of you will have the karma to move. Some of you will have the karma to stay. If you are in touch with your intuition you will be blessed with certainty, and that will take you where you need to go.

Mother Mary speaks. My children, this teaching of the Lamb in your heart, it is a new teaching. Take a moment and feel. The Lamb in your heart is an image of the vibration, of the metatronic Christ vibration, that is in the deep part of your heart around your soul structure. The Lamb is a beautiful image for what this vibration is. When we say to you, "Feel the Lamb," we are saying to you, "Feel this vibration in your own heart." It has a sound, and this sound might be "Maah, maah." So feel that. The wise ones go to the Good Shepherd or bring the Lamb to the Shepherd. So Mother Mary says,

> **Ye who want to be shepherds,**
> **go to the Shepherd and**
> **you will become what you meditate on.**

Mother Mary speaks. Yes, I do speak about My children in the area known as Yugoslavia. My appearances there in Medjugorje were to balance out the painful vibrations that were arising there. Much good work was done in Medjugorje, but the karmas were greater, and much suffering which could have been averted was not averted. But do not underestimate the value of My visitations and My appearances.

Your Mother Mary speaks. Soon one of the archangels will come, but we have more to tell you now. We want to talk to you about the *ecstasy of prayer.* Traditionally, spiritual life has been a path of distraction. The Gopis[8] were distracted by Lord Krishna. The monks that gathered around Shakyamuni the Buddha were distracted by his state of Nirvana. And the apostles and the many who came around Jesus the Christ were distracted by his Christ-Consciousness.

Please do not be too good for prayer.

Please pray for your fellow man, and in so doing you will know great joy and will be purified.

This is the constant message of Mary. And now I will step aside for the Archangel Metatron. And now you will feel the new vibration coming upon us.

◄ • ►

ARCHANGEL METATRON: Behold, Hosanna to the Highest! Whenever I come, I always proclaim the greatness of the God-Father-Mother-Son-Spirit Trinity. "Hosanna to the Highest" pervades the highest space and it opens up the doorways to the highest realms of the Divine Father-Mother God. And you may feel that opening happening now, above us, as the golden-yellow vibration with the whiteness above, opening up, with clarity.

Last week you were instructed to *pray*, to open to the Gold that is coming from the Father-Mother, the Highest Source. You were instructed to open your hands and receive the bounty that is being given at this time. We ask you to do that again. We ask you to cup your hands at a height between your heart and your throat, with eyes slightly turned up, and there will be the dispensation and the descent of a transmission now, and bliss now, that is coming down. You can feel this being activated. It has the quality of yellow streams of Gold that are coming down now.

Good. And now that your hands are full, we ask that you take your cupped hands and put them into your heart. And let the Gold fill your heart chakra. Let it spontaneously fill in the spots that need the Gold, so that you too will become rich. Now take your hands away and let the Gold shine above and below. It will shine up through your throat and mind and down below through your lower chakras that hold the vibration of your physical organs. And it will move spontaneously.

We ask you to be givers of the Gold. We ask you to go to the treasury house. And then we ask you to give the Gold, the coins, away. Not all of them, but some. And then go back to the treasury house.

We want you to be rich in spirit.

You will like this, and you will see the true source of bounty and delight. Remember the circle of giving and receiving. And then you will be agents of the living God. Metatron will now depart.

SOLANA: And now coming closer is Archangel Gabriel, full of present joy. Coming closer and closer, now blowing his trumpet. He's coming now very close. So may you all feel the perfected state that Gabriel always brings and announces.

* * *

ARCHANGEL GABRIEL: This could be described as the kingdom of God. All are welcome. All are welcome.

Archangel Gabriel speaks.

I am ever happy.

I am ever joyous.

Forever I announce the Perfected State that is the Divine.

And you, too, shall know and remember this. Not only those in this room, but those who may hear these words in the future. The Divine sits outside space and time. For now, space and time is a good medium [in which] to learn and to grow.

But outside of space-time is a vast reality of perfected bliss.

So, my little cherubs. Do not be afraid to blow your own trumpets. To remember your self and to announce that in your own field.

The sound of Gabriel, or a sound of Gabriel:

Hallelujah! Glory to God in the highest and forevermore.

Does not hearing these words make you *feel?* Hallelujah! Glory to God in the highest. This is medicine for all parts of your body and any part of your soul.

So I have a connection to you now, all of you in this room. I will be available to you in different times, in different places.

I am the clarion call.

I am the announcer of the perfected state. Heed my call and you will know the transmission that I speak of. I now depart you in love.

🌹

MOTHER MARY: Lord Mary speaks. I will now talk and teach about the *Cosmic Christ*. Within every manifested form is a duality, is yin and yang, positive and negative, male and female. This pervades the tissues and cells of the body. The coming of the Cosmic Christ is also a great teaching about the Christ nature that is feminine. This is good and timely. In the unity of the body, when the Christ energy can be harmonized—both male and female—then that physical form will learn about the unity of the feminine and masculine natures of Christ.

At first, it is good to feel the differences: to feel the vibration of Jesus, to feel the vibration of Mary, to feel their difference in qualities and how they affect your subtle structures and your physical structures. And allow yourselves to be guided by your intuition, to pray and to work with either aspect.

For those who are angry, let the vibration of Mother Mary comfort you.

For those that are frightened, let the clarity that is Christ-Jesus-Sananda strengthen you.

Open and experiment and ask in prayer, ask the Divine Father, the Holy Spirit that is the Mother, or the incarnate son, Jesus, who of those three is the best guide at this time for you. And let yourself be blessed and healed and anointed. And over time, let your whole body and inner structure be anointed, so that over time your physical body will change.

The blessings of the archangels are a unique contribution to the transmutation of the [physical] body and the subtle body into Christ-Consciousness. As has been taught, the different archangel empowerments affect the different chakras. Melchizedek, the first and seventh. Metatron, the second and sixth. Mikael, Lord Michael, the third and fifth. And always, the purity of prayer affects the heart chakra.

So, at first the Christ-Consciousness will be worked in individuals. And different individuals will be animated in different ways and purified in different ways. Some of you will carry a simplicity and may not even know [that this is happening]. Some of you will be more esoteric in function. It doesn't matter what the qualities are. What matters is the penetration and harmonization of the Christ-Consciousness in your structure.

Your Mother Mary speaks. Behold, the time of great changes is coming. Prepare yourselves. Open—open to the changes. Open to your own divinization. If your process of spiritual transformation is always one of reception and growth—*reception and growth*— then your integrity will be maintained. The Lamb is shown where to go by the Shepherd. So the Lamb receives the teachings, and the Lamb moves and grows. Now that you have the good fortune of [hearing] the revelation of the Lamb and the Shepherd, take the good advice and grow with the Shepherd.

The metaphors of the wolves and the lions that wish to eat the lamb, or the lamb wandering off and falling down a ravine or getting caught, are good metaphors for the karmas that exist. These karmas only exist ultimately to create safety and wisdom. Yes, the lamb shall grow into a ram, or a ewe, and there will be maturity, but first the lamb must be there. In this next period of time, in these next two to three decades, is the period of the lambs recognizing themselves and growing in the company of the Shepherd. There will be time in which the lambs, or some of the lambs, will mature into the rams and the ewes. And there will be a collective group. There will be—I'll say this again— there will be a time of the pairing up of rams and ewes in the form of men and women. This will be a common form. It will not be the only form, but it will be the primary form, of couples holding the male and female aspect of the Christ and teaching and working together. This will especially show up after the year 2015, but there will be signs of it before then. So, while two thousand years ago the position of the Christ was carried by Jesus alone at great cost, this time the position of the Christ will be carried by several hundred. A number that comes up often is 712. Many of these are being prepared now, and the signs are showing in them now.

These teachings will be difficult to receive by most of the people on Earth at this time. This is a higher teaching. It is not a teaching for bishops and prelates. It is not a teaching for war mongers who hide their enmity behind crosses bought with stolen money. It is not a teaching for those who wish to fulfill themselves through gluttony and indulgence and hope for cheap forgiveness with a Sunday at church. They have their own teachings and they will grow in their own time. But this will be a teaching for the elders. And the elders do not need the children to acknowledge them. For the acknowledgment is self-validating and shines through the heart and will be recognized by other elders.

So, Mother Mary says,

> **Please welcome My vibration into the deepest**
> **sanctuary of your heart.**
> **I am the very nature of the Christ Mother**
> **that is most intimate in your soul.**
> **I live there now.**
>
> **Come meet Me in the deepest sanctuary**
> **of your vulnerability.**
> **And My Son and the Divine Father meet us there too.**
> **We await you in our bliss.**
> **We invite you to dinner.**
> **Drink of our wine.**

Your Mother Mary speaks. Good night, Lambs of the World and those who love God. Your dreams and aspirations are for a great purpose. Let them be resolved in love, and directed by love, and alchemized by love, so that love becomes the final objective. And then your faith will be a burning reality that will light others on fire.

[All gathered sing "Hallelujah" 32 times in eight-bar melodic and harmonic phrases (to the melody of Pachelbel's Canon). Then they sing "ooh" or hum for two more of the same eight-bar phrases, then "Hallelujah" again for another eight-bar phrase, and then end softly.]

CHAPTER FIVE

Lambs of My Heart

MAY 30, 1996
MILL VALLEY, CALIFORNIA

Present: Fritz, Mitchell, Shelley, Devaka, Howard, and Solana.

SOLANA: Tonight we're in Mill Valley, California. We're going to do the invocation of the Hail Mary four times.

Hail Mary, full of Grace,
the Lord is with thee.
Blessed art thou amongst all women,
And blessed is the fruit of thy womb, Jesus.

Holy Mary, Mother of God,
Pray for us now, and forevermore.
Amen.
            [Repeated three more times]

❧

*M*OTHER MARY: Good evening, this is Mary.

SOLANA: She is addressing you all tonight as "Lambs of My Heart."

MOTHER MARY: Lambs of My Heart, the world is full of many different frequencies. Tonight, in the background, is music. This is actually a good sign, or a good example. Ah, and see here how the music disappears [as soon as we started to talk about it]—well at least is turned [way] down right there. It is a good sign that as you're trying to open and listen to the deeper prayers, the deeper frequencies, what happens? You hear a rock and roll song instead, and it distracts you from the pure attention to the higher prayer. Does that make sense? This is why it is traditional for people to leave the common world where there are many radios playing. And the radios are not simply Sony radios playing tunes, but the radios of common material themes, common streams, com mon thoughts. And so tonight as we're being a little subjugated to this other music, it is a sign for you of the influence of samsara, if you will, that will take your attention away from pure listening.

Mother Mary speaks. Children, the conflagration in Yugoslavia is growing. *It is growing.* I ask that you remember this part [of the world] in your prayers. On an historical level, the Balkans is the crossroads, has historically been the crossroads between Asia Minor and Europe. The Balkans has been the scene of warfare for many, many centuries. The Balkans is where the Great War [World War I] began. There was great fighting in the Balkans during World War II. It is a great area of karma and transmutation. And now, again, the Balkans is simmering. And so, not only are fellow humans suffering, but a key political place in your history, in your social politics, is also jeopardized. So we ask for you to remember this part of the world in your prayers because of the position this has on the greater political alliances and connections in your world. Whenever prayers are sent to an area they help many beings, and so secondarily praying for a country gives one great peace and a deeper compassion. That is the prasad of this prayer. So we ask you to remember this in your prayers.

My children, we've spoken a lot about the Lambs in your heart—*the Lambs in your heart*—and we want to refresh your memories on this. There are two parts of the prayer about the Lamb in your heart. The first part is allowing the recognition or the perception of the Lamb vibration in your heart. This can be aided by a vision, internal vision, of a lamb. It might also simply be a feeling of the tenderness of the lamb. This is a deep inner aspect of the heart chakra: the Lamb nature. We also discussed—I also discussed an esoteric meaning of the prayer of the rosary which is "Blessed is the fruit of thy womb, Jesus." The esoteric understanding is that "thy womb" refers to each individual's own personal heart, which is the womb of the soul and the Divine Person. And so, when you say the prayer, "Blessed is the fruit of thy womb," not only are you honoring Jesus of Nazareth and the feminine Christ—that is historical and cosmic—but you're also acknowledging the Christ within.

The first part, again, is the Lamb. The second part of the prayer is like a secret part of the prayer which is the *covering,* the covering of the Lamb. We described how the feminine aspect of the Christ-Consciousness has in large part the quality of covering, protecting. It is not smothering, it is a shielding—*it is shielding.* Allegorically, lambs need to be protected from the wolves. Lambs are easy prey for instinctive and carnal—for lack of a better word and not [placing] any connotation on this—primitive carnal desires of just instinctive living that is not integrated with the heart. That is the wolf in its negative sense: it is a carnal beast that is not connected to the heart. Now certainly the wolf can be connected to the heart, too. But, the wolf and the lamb—it means that.

Now, a higher part, an additional part of the prayer is of the Shepherd, the Staff of the Shepherd, and allowing the Lamb nature within to be shielded, protected, guided. This prayer is [given in] Psalm 23: "The Lord is my shepherd. . . . He leadeth me to [lie down in] green pastures." The verdant pastures, and so forth. There is an esotericism in there. For example, what is the green pasture? *The green pasture is the awakened chi in the body,* similar to the *parama* vibration that has been worked on with Mitchell, Solana, and so forth. So listen to that. "He leadeth me to green pastures." What does that mean? **You yourself become the green pasture. You become the vitality.** The green also relates to the heart chakra as well as the vitality of the whole body. The life, the vitality of the whole body. So this is a great prayer that can be used for your own serenity and your own *yearning.*

My children, there is good news. There will be a type of benediction that will be occurring. We're feeling that, and wish to communicate that, because of Divine decree some of the Earth's changes that are slated for 1997 and 1999 will not be as bad as they need to be. This is coming from very high Divine Father aspects of the unfolding. Now, more precisely, what does this mean for you all? Many of you have karmas to scatter from northern California. Northern California has been a place where many children of the light have gathered since the late '60s.

They've come, not only from the United States, but from all over the world to this place. They've been attracted to the higher vibrations that are permitted here. They've come here, it has been close to thirty years, and they've been able to meet one another, purify karma, learn, grow, handle some of the basics of life, purify their diet, have experiences of multi-dimensional consciousness, be able to meet one another, mate with one another, and so on and so forth. But, in the coding of this time, many of these children of light will now be leaving to go to new places to seed other communities. And this is in your fabric as well.

So, we ask you in the next nine months, especially, to meditate on this. Free will is always given—*free will is always given*. But we also wish you to meditate on your mission, on your purpose, on your agreements. For example, one of you might have the karma to set up community in central Idaho. This will help hold a beacon of light in that part of the country which still carries a lot of instinctive lower vibration. One of you might have the karma to help be in New Mexico or Texas, you see? And there are beings there that have agreements with you. So we ask each of you to appeal to combining with the highest good, the highest law, and the highest desire, so that you can combine and go to the best circumstance that is for you.

Now the time is also—might be not chaotic, but might be [described as] rumble-jumble. And it does not mean that you will leave California and go to one place and stay there. Some of you might go to two, or three, or four places. A few of you might travel around, even come back to California several years from now.

But this is a time of dispersion in the next few years. Just like the late '60s was a time of attraction to the [San Francisco] Bay Area, the '90s is a time of dispersion. And some of this began in the early '90s when the first indications of the Earth changes came. Many people left both Los Angeles and the [San Francisco] Bay Area for places such as Durango [Colorado] and the other centers—you know, in the West[ern states] especially. Now I want to talk about some of the karmas in Los Angeles.

Los Angeles is a city that is both good and bad. The strikes [riots] and fires that broke out a few years ago were certainly an indication for all to see of the incredible tension that exists in Los Angeles. Los Angeles is a city of tremendous duality. There is the greatest of wealth—you will see more Rolls Royces probably in Los Angeles than anywhere else in the world. There is also a city of great poverty. In your world, there is always duality—*there is always duality*. And in Los Angeles, there is a tremendous duality there and the friction is great. We have to say that Los Angeles is not the safest place to be in the next seven years. We recommend that if you have karmas in Los Angeles that you think about them very carefully. There might be great suffering in Los Angeles. Not to say a joke, but the City of Angels—you know in your world angels mean dead people. They are dead, and you see their spirit, which is an angel. That could be another way of describing the City of Angels [Los Angeles]—do you understand? Okay?

So again, there is always free choice. There is always a chance for redemption—even at the worst moment, there is a chance for redemption. But one also must be awake to karma and tendency and the reality of the practical circumstance. You must also be clear in your understanding of the difference between personal karma and group karma. A ferry sinks in Malaysia and five hundred people die. This is a group karma. The person who decides not to ride that ferry decides, "I am not going to share that group karma." Okay? Sometimes in ashrams there is a group karma that the individual might not have [and therefore they leave]. So, be sensitive to the difference between group karma and personal karma, because martyrdom is usually the payback of karma which is not necessarily holy in the eyes of the Lord, but may be a sacrificial act to pay back karma which could be paid back in a different way, without loss of life.

Behold, children, I bring you now Archangel Gabriel, and the vibration will now change.

* * *

ARCHANGEL GABRIEL: Now, this is Archangel Gabriel. Now you can see the difference in vibration. For those who have been coming week after week, you can feel the difference in the vibration. Last night Solana, Fritz, and Mitchell were talking about radiance. *The intuition of Gabriel is an intuition of radiance.* And as Fritz was describing, it is not a radiance that is a motivated radiance, or an efforted radiance, it is the effortless radiance that comes with the true abidance in a natural condition of the heart and of the devotional and spiritual personality. So feel the sense of radiance now, because the radiance that comes with Archangel Gabriel feels very three-dimensional. It fills all the cubic space in a perfect—there's a perfection that is here, a perfection. And it is from within the space that the incarnated Divine masters—the Jesuses of Nazareth, the Sai Babas[9] of Shirdi—it is within this radiance that they function in a world that is less than radiant. So enjoy this feeling. Let your body, the inner parts of your body—whether it is your ears, or your knees, or your throat, or your eyebrows, whatever part of your body does not feel perfect now—let the radiance move and make you clear, intelligent and peaceful.

Gabriel speaks. *What is the trumpet that I play?* What is the trumpet that I play? First, listen because it beckons to an internal trumpet, the trumpet some of the yogis call the *shabd* or the nada. That is part of the trumpet. Another explanation of the trumpet—when one is in deep samadhi, the "roaring of the breath" can be called the trumpet of Gabriel as well. This is Archangel Gabriel. I leave you now with a taste of the perfection of which I speak. Next the Archangel Metatron.

SOLANA: The darshan of Archangel Metatron has come to the higher realms above us right now. In the space here, roof-high, like a mother ship descending, is the darshan of Archangel Metatron, the Archangel of laughter as well as sweetness. The icon that you all use in the West of Santa Claus is a facet of Archangel Metatron. And in some sense tonight we're seeing a divinized, golden version of this aspect of Santa Claus, St. Nicholas, connected with Archangel Metatron. So now a dome of golden light is being radiated down through this circle around us. And for anyone listening to this tape or reading this information, a golden dome will be transmitted to you now.

[There was a pause of 10-15 seconds. The reader should also pause at this point.]

And we ask that you give thanks to the Glory that is God the Father, God the Mother, God the Spirit, the Trinity, the One in whom you appear, and in whom you disappear, the Great One, the One you know and will come to know, the Paradox of manifest existence and unmanifest existence.

◄ • ►

ARCHANGEL METATRON: Metatron speaks. Behold, be like the wise ones who stand on the outskirts of the city on a hilltop or mountaintop, as the waves sweep over the city. Watch the karmas be purified from afar. Be the elders who have heard the greater message of truth, who are willing to open to a cosmic process and not be dictated by the little dictator within that is endlessly chasing the teeniest and most insubstantial of temporary illusory consolations. So, be the watchers, and then be the ones that tend the holy lights so that others may come, be healed, be nurtured—the ones who heard half as well as you. And be a sign of the grace that you saw earlier so you may be an instrumentality of the Divine love.

It is a good time for the archangels. We have essentially veiled ourselves for hundreds or thousands of years so that mankind may go through its adolescence. Just like a loving parent lets go of his [or her] teenage daughter or son so that they can learn the lessons of adolescence, we have let go of humanity for the last two thousand years or so. But, like a good parent, we were ever watchful, ever prayerful, ever behind the scenes if we were needed. And truly and certainly, we came in times of great trouble. The stories of the archangels and the angels being intercessory or being intervening during World War I and in World War II, those stories are true. [Likewise] the stories of L'Archange Michel [Archangel Michael] in the battlefields of France during the Great War. And [likewise] the stories of the archangels in World War II [said in mystic circles to have been called upon to defend England during the Battle of Britain]. So, the careful parent makes sure that the teenagers do not self-destruct. The paradox of the suffering of an archangel is something that can basically not be described. But the shock of the lessons that were being learned during some of these worldwide conflicts was large even for us to see— if you understand this.

Therefore, I have given you gifts. **The Shepherd is the greatest gift.** Those who are willing to be shepherded can learn the way of the Good Shepherd and can be good shepherds themselves. It is the foolish lamb that wanders off before it is grown into a ewe, full of self-glamour. Nothing hurts the Shepherd more than to find [that] one of his lovely lambs has become supper.

In the name of all that is Good and all that is Divine, I leave you now, Archangel Metatron. I'll be back again to share with you.

❦

MOTHER MARY: Your Mother Mary speaks. The darshan of the Lord is ecstasy. The darshan of the Lord is samadhi. The darshan of the Lord is liberation. We ask you to permit yourselves the external ecstasies, because the path of internal ecstasies first is a path with many dangers involved. Even the saint Mother Meera[10] teaches that, in this time of the Kali Yuga, it is better to worship the external God. Why is this so? Why is this taught at this time? This is not taught to make you feel inferior. This is not taught to make you feel insignificant, a speck, insubstantial. This is not taught to demean you. This is taught because it is the easiest. It is taught because generally speaking it is the safest and it is the fastest [method of liberation] in this time of the Kali Yuga.

In ancient times things were different. Take ancient Vedic India —and yes, I, Mary, was alive in those times. I lived lifetimes among the Rishis, especially in the time period of 3200 BC until the 1300 BC era. I spent time preparing for My great incarnation as Mary, but I spent time with the Rishis. And in those times, there were cultures, small pockets, where the vibrational frequencies of the land were purified. Where Rishis would gather and hold what you might call the Advaita Vedantic vortex. Or—you could use the word—there were Rishis that held the Dharmakaya form, and the Dharmakaya form pervaded the valley, or the hillside, or the mountain. Therefore, others could come and "piggyback," if you will, and ride off that rarified essence that was held [there]. But, here in your time and your world, those rarified atmospheres rarely exist. There are a few teeny, the most tiny areas of your world where some of the great ashrams are, where this [rarified atmosphere] is held. Otherwise, the land is held by chaotic and erratic commercials, radio waves, all kinds of waves. Do you understand this? So, the [spiritual] message of the Kali Yuga is:

> "The Name of God" as prayers.
> Bhajan: chanting the Name of God to purify the throat.
> Darshan: the Vision of God via Guru or Deity.

All these things are good.

We wish to say a word about the Gurus because, at this time, at the time of the Kali Yuga, Gurus are splattered with manure. The Gurus in this time are among the greatest of Gurus because of the difficulty of holding dharma in this time. Look at the great ones that uphold the lineages in Tibet and Mongolia. Some of these are connected to the Eighty-Four Mahasiddhas.[11] There are six [Gurus] related to the Eighty-Four Mahasiddhas, that are holding dharma positions today. The ones in Tibet and Mongolia who have had to hold the dharma through times of secrecy, imprisonment, rape and pillage in the monasteries and nunneries, those are some of the great ones. The Mahasiddha who was the fisherman [actually the one who ate fish guts], Luyipa, he is one of these. He is one of the hidden older masters who has incarnated. He is what we call the equivalent of a seventh level old soul,[12] who skipped centuries of incarnation and came back as his final incarnation to hold this, finishing his last lifetime of a seventh level old incarnation.

The Gurus in the West, most of them, carry great fire, whether it is Gurumayi,[13] whether it is Sri Adi Da,[14] even [Swami] Muktananda.[15] But, now they carry great fire because of the purification that must be required and [because] of the negativity and the onslaught that they are faced with. They carry the fire to protect their bodies both physical and subtle, and to purify their space so they can hold their anchoring. It is a sacrifice to hold fire like this. So, for all those listening, the Guru function is a hellish function. It is a high service to dharma and to divinity. And we ask that you look at the life of Jesus, who was My son in that incarnation. His own people crucified him.

Mother Mary speaks. **Children, give me your sufferings. When you pray give me your pain, your anguish, your unfulfilled desires, and I will replace them with the purity of the Christ.** I want to instruct you in prayer. Face me when you pray. Do not hide inside yourself and hope I am listening. But face *Me* and see, *and see*—this is a truer form of intimacy. And at first you simply might see the wall, or the window, or the church pew in front of you. But as you face what you see, your eyes over time will rest. *Your eyes will rest.* And then you will see the palette of light in front of you in a new way. And then your vison will *deepen.*

Mother Mary speaks. **Children, I'll dry all your tears. I'll take them up and you will cry those tears never again. Come back, come back to the Heart of the Mother.**

CHAPTER SIX

I Am a Cosmic Glistening

JUNE 6, 1996
SAN RAFAEL, CALIFORNIA

Present: Lia, Fritz, Howard, Mitchell, Shelley, and Solana.

SOLANA: We will say the Hail Mary seven times to start the evening:

Hail Mary, full of Grace,
the Lord is with thee.
Blessed art thou amongst all women,
And blessed is the fruit of thy womb, Jesus.

Holy Mary, Mother of God,
Pray for us now, and forevermore.
Amen.

[Repeated six more times]

❦

MOTHER MARY:

In the Name of the Light I come.
In the Name of the *Christos* I come.
In the Name of the Father, of the Son,
of the Spiritus Eternal I come.
I am Lord Mary.
I am beyond the world.
My heart is ever present beyond the world.

What does this mean? What is this great mystery? What is this great secret of which I speak? The Hindu teachers have often spoken of this world as an illusion. What does that mean, that this world is an illusion? This world that could kill you. The streets that you cross with cars zooming by. They seem very real. The illusion affects your body. It can hurt you. It can kill you. It can bring you pleasure. So, what does it truly mean for Mary to say, "My heart is beyond this world"? Children, look deep within. That is why we meditate. To look deep within may take many, many years of your human time. But the admonition and the principle is still true. There is a reality that is prior to your perceptual experience. There is a greater reality.

Children, My heart is all-pervading as God's heart is all-pervading. I wish to share a secret with you. If you look at a black object, sometimes it appears *white* from the shadow glistening off of it. Sometimes it has other colors such as blue that glisten off the black nature. Likewise, when you look directly at the heart of God, sometimes you see a glistening color. When you look directly at the black—for example, the black obsidian stone— you see white or you see blue, but it is coming from a black source. Likewise, when you look at the heart of God you might see a color reflecting off that heart. You might see the blue that is Krishna. You might see the white that some call Vishnu. You might see the gold that is Christ or the soft blue that is Mary. You understand? *It is a glistening off the essential nature of the heart.* So, many confuse these glistenings for the true nature of the transcendental God Himself/Herself. But it is enough [even] to confuse it. You're still being distracted by the Light of the Father/Mother Self. And that can take you deep into the secrets of the Divine Reality.

So if your fellow men see the blue of God and worship Krishna, then let them be distracted by God in that way. If your fellow men simply feel the blackness, the impersonalness, which many call Allah, then let them worship in that way. And let your fellow brothers and sisters be distracted by what is distracting them.

As Mary, as Lord Mary, I am a cosmic glistening throughout the cosmos.

My essential nature is that of the Father.

This is a great mystery and paradox for you who seem to feel separate from that which is the Divine Reality. When you close your eyes and see the zigs and zags of light and the sparks, this is one way to contact the reality that is beyond this world. It is also a great practice to contact the reality that is beyond this world while fully perceptive of this world. This is why people are taught prayer and instruction.

I wish to tell you a secret. Energy flows out of your eyes. If you meditate and you are still, you will realize that energy is flowing out of your eyes instead of your eyes simply resting in your skull, simply resting. But instead, energy flows out, usually out of one eye more than the other through a focus of our attention. So as we begin to come to rest through spiritual practice, through bodily purification, we will see that our eyes begin to rest. As our eyes begin to rest our vision will improve. We will start to see what is to the side of us, and even perhaps to what is behind us. We will start to see perhaps into subtle worlds and to what is beyond the subtle worlds. You may feel even, at some point, that the visions that you see are no more than glistenings of light on your eyeballs yourself; and that there is no reality whatsoever to depth perception. That is why some teachers say, "I am eternally in one place." The Guru Adi Da says, "I am eternally in one place contemplating my own bliss." This is an example of one whose eyes are at perfect rest, knowing that even when he moves through time and space he, his essential nature, is not moving at all. And perhaps many of you have had that experience in which you are moving through an apparent visual reality but you're not moving whatsoever.

Children, let me tell you God is *feeling and knowledge*. *God is feeling and knowledge.* Many are deluded by the knowledge that they have. But, they do not know feeling. Some are deluded by feeling only without knowledge. Children, **come up, come up in your feeling and come up in your knowledge.** And then that will settle back into the temple of your body and the temple of your heart. One of the things we say to you in these evenings, is that these evenings are not simply information. They are not simply words. They are not simply a look into a book of knowledge or encyclopedia. Hidden within these sessions is the *transmission* as well as the feelings. These are activated through hearing. The ears are also a means to feel. *The ears are also a means to feel.*

I, Lord Mary, carry a great weight. The burdens and sufferings of this world can only be carried by the Divine personalities. Much like a school teacher can carry the safety of thirty other school children—making sure they get on the bus safely and are returned home to their mothers at night—likewise I, Mary, carry the karmas of billions under My cloak. Likewise, *I can help carry your burdens, too.*

Now I wish to talk a little about childish religion versus real religion. At first, you can give me your sufferings like a child. And at first, that is okay. But your growth is continually monitored like a mother watches the growth of her child and teaches responsibility. So, at first, if you need to respond childishly that is okay. And for many, it is the hardest thing to do first, to respond like a child. Do not be afraid that you will be kept a child in the heart of God.

Lord Mary speaks. The times of tribulations are in the near future. You will likely witness tribulations occurring between now and the end of the century. These tribulations are karmic purifications. They're like the student who gets a D+ at the end of the year. Why at the end of the year do some students receive A's, and some receive D+'s or F's? It is not that God is unfair. It is that the lesson was ignored. Does this make sense? Likewise, karmic times of tribulations is report card time. And some will be getting D+'s and F's, and will take the course again.

Lord Mary Speaks. Prepare yourselves. *Prepare yourselves.* And how can you do this? First, tend your own fire. *Tend your own fire.* What does this mean? In the body the fire is in the navel. Many teachers and many cultures have taught, "Cultivate the fire of the navel." There are many ways to do this. There are physical exercises, yogas, tai-chi's, Taoist exercises, that do this. There are also methods of prayer that do this. Some of these methods of prayer involve visualizing a fire in your navel. And it is centered right in the area between the second and third chakra, so that the fire between the liver and the spleen, or the left and right sides of the intestines, is balanced. Many of you have the fire on one side of your body, primarily on the right side, or the liver side. It is a great health practice to balance the sides of your fire.

First, we're going to talk about the "green pasture" that we talked about last week. Last week we spoke about following the shepherd to the green pasture, and that the green pasture also means the vitality, the chi, the green, the vibration. Likewise, that green vitality [what Solana calls the fourth dimensional energy, and which the acupuncturists call the *chi*], this pervades that whole region, also, of the intestines, the spleen, and the liver. You can take your hand and make a great circle around that whole space. If you look at Solana's body you can see. [From] the spleen to the left, [this energy] goes all the way down to the second [chakra], to the liver, up to the third [chakra]—that whole area right there. You can reverse it the other way. You can prepare yourselves by purifying the green vibration, the fourth dimensional energy, the fourth dimensional vibration in this part of your body. This will bring you health, vitality and longevity. In your prayers when you pray to the Shepherd, "Leadeth me to green pastures—may You leadeth me to green pastures," the "green pastures" doesn't necessarily mean a good job, or a nice place to live. Esoterically it means the green pastures within your own body—*the green pastures within your own body*. These are purified primarily through diet—*purifying diet*. It can later be purified through prayer and visualization, especially [the visualization] that the liver and spleen are balanced, and that the second and third chakras are balanced. This is like a [Christian] cross, you see, between the liver and spleen. You can even visualize [something] like a green cross in that part of your body, you see. If you visualize that now—we'd like each of you listening to this tape to visualize this cross now. The horizontal [part of the cross] is between the liver and the spleen, which is just below the rib cage and basically touches the ribs. And then the [vertical part of the] cross [can be visualized] from the third chakra basically down, you could say, to between the second [chakra] and the first [chakra]. If you visualize this in your own space you should see that the cross is not perfect. If you really tune in and visualize you will see that perhaps the horizontal beam is at a funny angle, or it is higher or lower, or it is aimed in a different direction. Or, the green is not perfectly beautiful, up and down, side to side. Do you see this? Also, that the vertical axis is not purely straight. If you visualize this and practice with it in your prayer, then this will be a great practice for you. Take a minute to feel this. *[The reader is invited to engage this exercise.]*

We're going to do a visualization. Visualizing the Lamb in the heart. *Visualizing the Lamb in your heart.*

Now, visualize Christ, Lord Sananda, taking the Lamb down to the cross *[just discussed]*.

And now, the Lamb is residing in the place where the cross meets.

And now, Christ assumes the position on the cross.

And the color and the vibration of the cross is green.

This is a great esoteric prayer. This prayer might take a few years to perfect. It could typically take ten months to six years to perfect this.

Now, I wish to talk about baptism. Baptism by *water,* and baptism by *fire.* We will dissolve this color green, this cross—that visualization will dissolve.

[And now, the baptism by water.]

Go back to your heart, where the Lamb is in the heart.

And now, you will visualize Mary in your heart.

And now, Mary will lead you to the water.

And Mary leads you down to the cross.

And now, the cross is navy blue.

Solana calls this the fifth dimensional energy. It is the water. It is the water of the deep lake; it is a baptism.

This will be stimulated slightly now with everybody present here. That fifth dimensional energy, you will feel it on the posterior fontanel, the rear fontanel, back of your head. Where the flat of your head and the back of your head meet are two soft spots. That is the gateway for this baptism. Those two soft spots there. That area will be stimulated just a little bit for everybody present here.

And now, Mary stays on the cross. And the Lamb, which is your essential nature, is at the junction of the cross. And this is the Shepherd leading you to water. And as a touch of the nature of water baptism. This is a higher, more intense practice which is mostly effective if the green pasture meditation has been perfected. So please feel this. And you can feel now, especially, that the horizontal bar between the spleen and the liver is not balanced yet. Let the vibration of Mary and the water move into the spleen and liver and gently, for a minute, wash it. It will cool down the fires and purify. And now I will stop this. Now I will let this visualization dissolve.

And now, the baptism by fire.

The baptism by fire has different possibilities—*has different possibilities.* We're going to give you one possibility now.

Now, you have visualized the Lamb at the heart.

And now, the Lamb descends to the cross.

And the color of the cross is a light blue, but not a sky blue. It is the type of blue that comes from a Bunsen burner, or a gas flame, you see?

Solana often refers to this as like a seventh dimensional vibration. And now, there will be a slight stimulation of this vibration in you. And this is a much higher burning purification. This is a taste of baptism by fire in the body. *[A pause for a few seconds.]* Now, we will stop. That is enough of that one.

Let all that vision dissolve. I want everybody to open their eyes now for a second to break that. These are esoteric Christian yogas based on that prayer of "The Lord is my Shepherd." These were taught anciently, and they are essentially forgotten at this time. But these are practices one can [still] do. And I am sure you all felt the power and the potentiality of these prayers. It is like a Christed yoga. And at the right time the baptisms will be made more intense and purified. It is like a piece of meat. You don't throw a piece of meat on 800-degree fire. It doesn't cook right. You need the right temperature and the right time for cooking. So those who rush into rapid spiritual experience become, we will say, overcooked meat—no good, okay? So this is a way to prepare yourself. There are other yogas, too, involving the higher chakras. You can imagine them. However, the importance of creating the foundation is a great matter. And the base is like a triangle—the base must always be greater than the apex. Likewise, build from the bottom up, and then the work that is done on the higher levels will be permanent.

Mother Mary speaks. My children, please practice these meditations. These are secret meditations. Some of you will really see the value of them, the esoteric value of them. Please practice them until they're perfected and then there will be others [meditations] for you to have. Then you will be prepared yourself. Mother Mary had said, "Prepare yourself." By preparing yourself individually, you will be of greater effect in preparing your family, your friends, and the group that you are with.

In the name of the Father, the Son, and the Spiritus Aeternus. I take My leave at this time. And now Archangel Gabriel will come.

* * *

ARCHANGEL GABRIEL: The fanfare of Gabriel is here. I announce the perfection of the Divine moment—the peacefulness and the naturalness of Divine realization. My call is a paradox. My call is to announce something that is coming, and my call is to announce something that has come. You have two hands. In the left hand is held that which is to come. In the right hand we are holding that which is already here. Then the two hands are put together at the heart. So, the paradox is held in the nature of the heart. Thus, we can stay in the place of the manifest and the unmanifest, knowing that at the heart. *[During this communication the audiotape had run out.]*

SOLANA: At this point I am going to simply repeat, as I remember it, what Archangel Gabriel said, so that it is not lost on the tape. What happened after this was that Gabriel announced the sounding of the trumpet. And in the instant that Gabriel said, "The trumpet will sound now," there was suddenly a *beep, beep*— a truck honked that exact second right outside our door, in an evening that has been basically very silent! And we all laughed at that moment. Then we felt the kundalini rise in us, which was the sound of the trumpet. That is essentially what Gabriel had said, and then Gabriel left. Now, it is time for Archangel Metatron, and we will resume the communication.

Feel the vibration of Metatron. There is a golden disk of 24 feet [in diameter] that is now floating above the circle here. It is slightly concave, the disk above us. And from this disk are gentle filaments of gold that are coming down over this group. You are now getting more and more sensitive to the different vibration between Metatron, Mary, and Gabriel. What is this golden disk that has appeared before you? Essentially, it is a disk that has been co-created through the process of Archangel Metatron and through the process of the six who are here tonight to form a vortex for transmission and communication. So you have co-created this temple. And for those who are listening to or hearing this material, whenever you gather in a group, a form of a temporary temple of light is always made. And if the intention is for a higher purpose, then a higher temple will be created.

◄ • ►

ARCHANGEL METATRON: I am Archangel Metatron. What is my sign? What is my vibration? I'll show you. Take an image, an emanation of this gold disk, and put it in your heart chakra—

like a four-inch disk that is descending from the circle of gold. And now they're being inserted, wafer-thin, into your heart chakra. Perfectly circular—feel that vibration. I am Archangel Metatron, archangel of love, of Divine love. This is my vibration. It is the perfect circular left and right, up and down. The love shown by the gold is balanced and pure. I am Archangel Metatron. Feel the vibration. Let it be an essence of a hologram that is in your heart, a pure template. And you can feel the vibration that is in you.

I am Archangel Metatron. I speak: Behold, the glory and the majesty of Sananda-Christ is *just on the other side of your perception.* Look—*look* beyond the golden disk that is above you. And look beyond the golden disk that is in your heart. And there you will see the outreaching arms of Christ, smiling to you, inviting you to eternal embrace. I am the sign of the eternal embrace of Christ. I am Archangel Metatron. Now, each one of you will experience this at this time.

We will go to a visualization above the golden disk. Starting with Howard, rising above the golden disk—then Mitchell, Shelley, Solana, Lia, and Fritz. And now we stand in our subtle higher form above the disk. Please visualize this. And now Howard will start first. Howard will turn around and a few feet away will see the form of Sananda-Christ, and move a few feet towards Him. [*To Howard:*] Close your eyes and feel the heart-embrace *now,* and lose yourself in that embrace until there is no Howard or separate Christ. And now, Mitchell, turn around, and within two or three feet of you is the embrace also. And the arms of Christ go over your shoulders and you hold Him down below the waist. And you're merged at the heart, merging, feeling at the heart. And now, Shelley—but, Shelley, for this exercise you will turn and see Mary. And you turn and Mary embraces you. And all your anxieties are just given to Her at the heart. And Lia, you join them. You join Shelley and Mary. And Fritz, now, you turn. And when you turn, I see you kneel on one knee first. And Christ takes your hands and raises you up. And you put your hands over His shoulders and His arms around your waist. And He holds you until you can't see Him, and a golden vibration of indefinable feeling merges into your heart. And now, Solana *[silence on tape as Solana is initiated into this process]*.

Having sat in this meditation for a minute, we will slowly move it back to our sense of subtle individuality, having known that we have merged into a sense of Christ-Consciousness. And now the six of you will face one another in that subtle vision and link hands together. And we'll also do it on the physical. So, put your hands out like this *[Solana leads group by extending his hands to the sides of his body, palms open and facing forward at shoulder level]*, so our hands touch together. Six is a holy number. Gathering in sixes and twelves is an esoteric form of gathering. Now, let's separate. And we'll come back down to our body. Solana will speak of the Star of David, listening to the words of Metatron.

The Star of David ✡

The Star of David is a sacred geometry. It is two 3's. It refers to many things. There are many mysteries and subtleties within the Star of David. It is not simply a picture that David liked a few thousand years ago. But it refers to the sacred nature of two 3's, of 6. Most simply, if you sit in groups of six, especially three men and three women, you will be able to create spiritual Stars of David, magical Stars of David, and use these for healing purposes.

I am Archangel Metatron. I have given you much to contemplate. Use these teachings and enjoy the bounty of the Lord.

🌹

MOTHER MARY: Lord Mary returns. My children, many are the gifts that you've received tonight. Gifts of practice, and strengthening, gifts we hope you will use and enjoy, and perhaps teach others. These gifts will help you not only individually, but will help others in preparing and learning of the way of the Cosmic Christ. I have spoken all that is needed to be spoken tonight. In the Name of the Christ, in the Name that is All, that is pure and already clean, of virtue, I am Lord Mary in eternal service.

CHAPTER SEVEN

Right Through the Star
JUNE 13, 1996
SAN RAFAEL, CALIFORNIA

Present: Lia, Howard, Shelley, and Solana.

❦

*M*OTHER MARY: Congratulations. This is Mother Mary speaking. We have completed the first leg of the instructions for the coming of the Cosmic Christ. There will be more instruction later on. But much material has been given in these last six weeks. **We pray and we urge that at least some of you will take these practices on and then teach them to others.** Some of this teaching reflects ancient esoteric wisdom that was taught in some of the Christian mystery schools. And some of this information is newer, updated for your time. The information about *the prayer of the crosses* in the lower chakras is a type of esoteric Christian yoga that has very rarely been experimented with. We hope that some of you, and we're especially thinking of Lia, will choose this as a path. For the others, it is their path if they're interested. But we urge Lia to take a good look at doing this path. For it will be very healing for her and purifying for her, especially for some of her life's work that lies ahead. We wish for you to know that there is a mood of happiness surrounding the completion of this course. The information that is on this tape is not only educational in terms of word knowledge, but it is educational in terms of vibrational knowledge. I wish to talk a little bit about what we mean by vibrational knowledge.

Scripture becomes dead when the vibrational knowledge is lost. Now, truly the vibrational knowledge can only be carried and understood by aspirants and holders of more maturity. In ancient times, and in authentic traditions, the elders were really the ones that held the vibrational knowledge. In certain traditions, such as the Tibetan traditions, an elder could be recognized as a young infant, or a young child, because the elders who were of older physical age could still tell by esoteric yogic signs that such a one carried the vibrational knowledge. But in today's world it is extremely common that the vibrational knowledge is forgotten, or is placed at such a lesser importance that the word "knowledge" is held to be sacrosanct.

This is not the true picture. The true picture is that *love is the way*. Christ is *love*. Christ is a lover, is not a knower, in His primary essence. So if theology was complemented with respect for vibrational knowledge, then the traditions would be purified. However, this is in general not the case at this time. Another thing we wish to say—and this is part of the work that Archangel Metatron has especially been active[ly engaging] with a tiny select group of people over the last few years—is to activate the angelic, or what Solana calls the sixth dimensional, vibration—to activate this in the lower chakras, and especially in a non-celibate tradition—because traditionally these chakras have been activated in a celibate monastic path, which has its limitations. One of the limitations is simply that, for religious aspirants, the celibate path is not the path for all, but perhaps just the path for some. So part of the experiment of this time is that the angelic vibration be activated in the lower chakras. Now we wish to comment on this further.

Two thousand or so years ago, when the Lord Jesus Christ made his appearance as Christ and his demonstration of the Christ power, he demonstrated many things. He demonstrated, certainly, the power that love could have over pain and death. But he also demonstrated *ascension,* radical ascension, rejuvenation of the physical body. We wish to talk about what occurred after the death of Christ. In order to understand this fully, we need to talk about the concept of parallel universes. Imagine a deck of cards. A parallel universe is like a card in a deck. So, in your reality now, you are one card in the deck. There are parallel universes stacked on top and below your universe and on other sides, just like a deck of cards. Through esoteric means [understood by Solana and others], these parallel universes can be entered into and yoga [spiritual work] done there and purification done there. For example, there is a parallel universe where the man known as Adolf Hitler, who led the Third Reich, [was victorious, and] the Third Reich won the war. There is a parallel universe where this occurred. There is a parallel universe where the Confederacy won the Civil War. And so forth.

In your parallel universe, it was the karma and the choice of our Lord and Savior, Jesus Christ, to physically perish on the cross—*in your parallel universe*. However, he was in a Transcendental God-state during the time of the crucifixion, in which he had transcended identification with the physical body—and in which, in essence, his soul could walk in and out of his physical body at will. This was not only a high yogic attainment, but an attainment that accompanied such an Infinite Soul. So to repeat that this is not only a high yogic accomplishment which yogis can, and have, accomplished, but it is also a gift of one who has supreme identification with the Divine Reality. So, when the Lord Jesus Christ died on the cross, *it was a type of bequeathal.* It was a type of demonstration—his gift to demonstrate that love is greater than death—and this was the ultimate demonstration of it.

However, his ascension was not in material, third-dimensional reality, but his ascension was in subtle form—in a subtle reality which, through his abilities, could pierce the third-dimensional reality and be demonstrated. So his subtle form could be perceived. During the three days of the burial the guards were drugged by some Jewish peasant girls who flirted with them and gave them some wine. And the tombstone was rolled away by several men and the body was taken away. Nicodemus was also involved in this. The tombstone was rolled back and the Roman guards suspected something in the morning. But they covered it up. They didn't know for sure. [*They were afraid of being punished so they kept silent—Solana.]* The physical body itself—there was a burial ceremony in which the body was burned. Mary Magdalene was present at this, along with a select group of initiates. There were many flowers around the corpse when this was done. This was a very high sacred ceremony. Now, the subtle body of Christ did appear as is said in the New Testament. And because of the power of Christ's identification with the Divine Reality and his Realization, his projection of it in time and space was very apparent—it was very, very clear. However, it was of an etheric nature.

In other parallel universes, Christ did not die on the cross. Christ was taken out early on the cross and was convalesced and regenerated through his yogic regeneration powers and through the help of certain healers. There was an esoteric woman healer-teacher, who was one of the women who, once Jesus's body was rescued from the tomb, particularly was adept at reactivating his kundalini and reactivating his life-force as if it was stored, sort of, in cold storage. And Christ then, in this [other] parallel universe, did travel off to the East.

There are more distant parallel universes in which Christ also survived the cross and did make travels to England and America. But these were in parallel universes, not in this universe.

But we did want to talk to you a little bit about what actually happened here. The true demonstration of Christ's death was not what the common fundamentalist orientation is, clearly enough. **But it is the demonstration simply that love transcends death, that love is a greater realization than death.** And that if done perfectly, or near-perfectly, there is a miraculous realization of identification beyond the physical body. The point is not exactly the history of "Did this happen?" and proving this or proving that. This information that we're giving is [what is] coming through at this particular time. And it is truly not a known. It will never be proven. It is not something that can ever be proven. This is the information that we are giving at this time. It is for your benefit. You can do what you want with it. But what you do with it, we urge you to—and this is for all the listeners of the tape. The point is not to argue what did happen—that is of some interest—but the main point is to understand the *gesture* that Christ made at this time.

Now, one reason why we talk about this is because Christ's physical body was a highly refined yogic vehicle. I'll say it again—*was a highly refined yogic vehicle*. Not only did he practice yogic practices in earlier lifetimes, but he also practiced certain yogic practices in that lifetime where he was Jesus.

And part of his practice is one that we're going to share with you now. And this has to do with—it is going to take a minute to come through on this—the first practice. There are a few practices. The first practice has to do with the Star. In the New Testament it talks about Christ's teaching about the [Morning] Star. The Star is actually an esoteric portal to the higher universes. And we wish to share a meditation now at this time, for this to be contacted.

For all those present, we want you to visualize the space that is known as the pineal gland which is in the area, you could say, in the back of the third eye area.

Imagine a jaw-breaker type, maybe one-and-three-quarter-inch diameter golden sphere in that space.

Imagine a *gold* sphere that is perfectly round and smooth [in the area of the pineal gland].

Now that that is held, visualize the adrenal glands. The adrenal glands are on the inside of the kidneys near the spine. Visualize the adrenal glands also as that size, but closer to a quarter-inch to half an inch.

And we will be working with four colors. The inner color is *black*, pea size, solid black, left and right [adrenals], surrounded by *white* of maybe an eighth of an inch [in thickness]. The next is *gold*, maybe one thirty-second of an inch in thickness—and then a *sky blue*. Black, white, gold, sky blue—visualize those in your left adrenal and your right adrenal.

Spend a few seconds and visualize them.

This is one of the practices that Jesus practiced and taught eso-terically. The practice was given to him in the area now known as Pakistan, when he was traveling there in his teens, through a master that he had past-life contact with, who was an adept of a different tradition. *Black, white, gold, sky blue.*

Now, an X [formation] is made. The vibration triangles to an apex in the center of the heart chakra. [The adrenals form the bottom points of the X, and the heart chakra is the junction of the X.] *Bright red* [is the color for the center of the heart chakra]. This can be activated with a Tibetan syllable [pronounced] "fut," that is transliterated as "Phat" in the English language. *Phat. Bright red,* heart chakra, Phat.

Then, the X clicks up, X's out to each ear where the *duplication* is made of the *black, white, gold, sky blue.* And this is in the inner ear within half an inch, as far as you can stick your finger in, within half an inch.

You can hold that vibration [for a little while].

You can see that this is a practice which takes time to develop. Because if you're doing it correctly the first time you will see the difficulty in holding those colors and holding it balanced in both left and right ear. **If you're doing it right, you will see that you're doing it wrong at first.** Does this make sense to every-body? Okay. But [continue] holding the intention.

Then, through activation by transmitter at the heart, these four points are activated [even] more through the power of that red vibration at the heart. So hold the [energy] field. What will begin to happen is that a vibration will arise from the left adrenal to the left ear and from the right adrenal to the right ear just in a line directly up. As this intensifies, it will create a triangle with the gold sphere that is in the pineal. [The three points of this new triangle are the inside left ear, the inside right ear, and the pineal gland.]

It will intensify and intensify, and then it will reach the point where that golden sphere is launched. And it launches out into the subtle realm. And the doorway to the subtle realm will be perceived as either a low setting star, or it will be perceived as a part of the sun at sunset where only part of the sun is available. And the consciousness goes *directly* towards either the little star or the very top of the sun that is on the horizon.

We will do this now if it hasn't been in place.

In the Name of the Divine Father, the red vibration is activated.

In the Name of the Son, the adrenal points are activated.

In the Name of the Mahashakti, Divine Mother, the vibration is raised up to the ears.

These are integrated. Intensity is forced to the gold. And now the launching occurs.

And let the launching go directly with simple focus, with pure focus.

The focus must be pure and trusting, right through the Star, or that point on the sun.

Go directly through that and then go through into the place on the other side.

Hosanna, hallelujah, praise to the God in the highest.

And you glimpse the higher Father realms at this point.

And receive blessings and gifts to bring back.

You will stay there for the time that is right. Then, you will return with the gifts or prasad from this.

Now, some or all of you will be returning. As you return, let the golden sphere come to gentle rest back in its initial spot. Let it cool down. Let it rest. Let it be welcomed back in a *feminine* gesture.

Let your body receive it, nurture it, cool it down and slow it down, and hold it. As you do this you will feel any transmission of heat or velocity move in through the body as the gift of receiving this. And let that move into the body as it will, to heal and nurture the body. And then let the vision of the gold sphere dissolve.

And then let the vision and the feeling of the points in the ears dissolve.

And let the vision and the feeling of the points in the adrenals dissolve.

So maybe now there is just the feeling of the red in the heart, which is still held by that Tibetan syllable "Phat." And now let the red begin to permeate the whole body, dissipating slowly. And it fills the body with a warmth and strength. So when it fills the whole body it simultaneously dissolves. And you are left feeling empowered, activated, purified, gifted.

So, My children, you have received a few great prayers. We're going to remind you of some of them.

You have received the prayer, *A Blessing for the Earth,* in the earlier parts of our discourse. This is a prayer that will bless you as you bless the world.

You have received *The Prayer of the Lamb in Your Own Heart.* This will activate the Christ-nature within you and also help you cultivate the Divine Mother/Christ aspect in your own self.

You have also received the gift of the esoteric understanding of the parts of the prayer of being led to greener pastures and being led to water, in those prayers of the lower chakras with the crosses of green and blue *[The Prayer of the Crosses].*

And now you've received a great gift, a high prayer, a prayer known to the esoteric initiates of Jesus the Christ. And a prayer that he had been taught and was a master of. And we will call this prayer *The Prayer of the Divine Return.* The Prayer of the Divine Return.

We wish to talk a little bit about what this name means. On the one hand you are returning to an inner harmony in your own body structure and esoteric structure. That is one type of return. Another return is that you're returning to the Divine Father realms. And also, you're divinely returning back to your individual form. So there are three returns in this. *The Prayer of the Divine Return.*

Mother Mary speaks. My children, I am going to take leave now at this time to let the two other Archangels speak.

* * *

ARCHANGEL GABRIEL: Ah, hah! It is I, Lord Gabriel, the trumpet player. I am not only one who plays the trumpet, but I am a player, a Divine player. Thus, I am a trumpet player. And I am happy in perfect service to the Divine Will and Law. I say to you *call,* call to the Lord. Call to the Lord through the Lord's Agents of help. Call to those who you resonate with. Call to those whose glistenings shimmer to you and whose colors you need at that time. Like a common musician, if you ask me to play a song I will play a song for you. But my song will be a Divine song.

I am the bearer and proclaimer of the Good News of that which is here, and that which is to come. Feel free to pray to me to hear my song, for I am *Empty.* And, the prayers go directly through me to the very heart of God Himself/Herself. I am Archangel Gabriel and I leave you now. And I leave you with this transmission which will be transmitted in the silence. *[A spiritual activation of radiance is given to everyone present in the circle.]*

I am Archangel Gabriel, and before I leave there is one last thing I wish to say. Please listen well to the words of the Mother, Divine Mother Mary. **Receive these prayers as gifts and rise up with them.** That is all.

SOLANA: And now, Mother Mary returns.

MOTHER MARY: Greetings My children. I, Lord Mary, have a message to you from Metatron.

Metatron had said, "My golden lambs, last time when I was with you I gave you the highest teachings that I could give you. I gave you the means to merge with the Christ. Remember that. Remember the golden disk that appeared above and then that was placed in your heart. Remember how we rose up through the disk and turned and were embraced by Christ. This is a sacred mystery. *Please practice this.* And once you have learned this I will teach you more. I am ever in the service of the heart of God. I am, for many, the answer to prayers. I leave you with the bliss that you have felt before through me."

This is the message that Archangel Metatron gave to Me, Lord Mary, to share with you at this time.

So, we wish to conclude. We will say this:

Become light bearers.

If you hold the light,

And practice holding the light,

**And are willing to share the light
through service and prayer,**

The light will spontaneously raise you up.

**And then you will know a delight and an enjoyment
of being in the chain of grace**

That comes from the heavenly abode of the Divine.

Consider practicing these prayers; perfect them.

Let the light move in your body and beyond and be Christed.

And then, not only will you know more of the Cosmic Christ,

**But you will add to the momentum of
the return of the Cosmic Christ,**

And be part of the Cosmic Christ itself.

In eternal service, I am Mary.

*   *   *   *   *   *   *

SOLANA: This is Solana speaking, and I want to do a little commentary on The Prayer of the Divine Return, as a guide for those who wish to practice this. First of all, the meditation involving the kidneys is a very important meditation. And if you practice The Prayer of the Green Cross in the lower chakras, once that becomes stronger, then you can let the vibration of the green cross move backwards through your body to help purify the kidneys. Okay?

That prayer spoke a lot about the spleen and the liver, as you recall, where the horizontal bar [of the cross] rests. However, the kidneys are kind of *the hidden*. You know I have been experimenting with the concept, which I think is probably accurate, that the kidneys represent the [psychological] "shadow." The left kidney is the female shadow and the right kidney is the male shadow. The right liver is more of the, I call it the light male, and the spleen, more of the light female. And they relate to the different quadrants of the aura. But the karmas [relating] to the dark female are in the left kidney and [the karmas relating to] the dark male are in the right kidney. And once you begin to purify the karmas more "up-front" [in the spleen and liver, light female and light male, then] we can deal with the karmas behind [in the left and right kidneys, dark female and dark male].

So if that prayer is established, then we can allow purification to go on in the kidney structure. And it can be worked with both the green cross and the blue cross. But there is a great healing that takes place there. This is something I was working on as a theory, and then I had also seen it in Chinese medicine. I have been feeling that the kidneys are the key organs for longevity, for balanced and very profound kidney health is the key to longevity. I had been working with this, and then I read in a Taoist book a few weeks ago that this is what the Taoists say as well. So this is a type of prayer yoga that can be done. And once, truly really, *truly really* it takes, the more purified one is in the green and the blue [vibrations], then the more profoundly *The Prayer of the Divine Return* can happen.

Let's talk about the visualization of those colors. *Black, white, gold,* and *sky blue* relate to different dimensions and different aspects. And there are yogas that those different four colors represent that can be activated too. But on a simple level, if one is feeling tired, on a psychic level there will be "female" energy in your left adrenal and "male" energy in your right adrenal. In other words, let us say your mother-in-law is visiting and she is just "in your space" and you're tired. You will find her psychic energy in your left adrenal. So women's psychic energy will be picked up in your left adrenal, and men's psychic energy in your right adrenal. By flushing those areas with gold or white [light], it will return that psychic energy back to those people. This is one way in meditation that you can see who are you carrying—who is in your [psychic] space. It is a very interesting meditation. It is very important to ground those energies in those organs.

Now let's discuss the activation in the heart. This practice is typically taught now in the Tibetan Buddhist tradition, especially in the Red Heyagriva tradition. And the Red Heyagriva is a wrathful protector—*the Red Heyagriva.* And of course, it is an esoteric tradition that was taught certainly before Tibetan Buddhism arose. But today it is most available in that tradition, if that makes sense to you. And for those who wish to study you can look at Tibetan iconography, at *tangkas* of Red Heyagriva, and you will get a sense of what that vibration is that is being activated.

Moving up to the ears, there is some more esotericism there. The points moving up through the ears move up through the thyroid [pulses]. There are thyroid pulses on either side of the neck. And as it moves up into the ears there is a spontaneous balancing of the thyroid system. For many people the thyroid system is really out of balance, especially in the navy blue color of the fifth dimension. Most thyroid disorders, either hyper- or hypo-thyroidism, have to do with a real imbalance in the thyroid functioning. And practicing this prayer is a way to start to balance the thyroid. So if any people here who are listening have thyroid issues, this prayer will help that. And then *listen* [to your intuition], with those [psychic] points in the ears. These practices can really be studied for months. And part of the listening process will also be to listen to what is in there, things that are processed and unprocessed. A lot of us don't really hear or process what we hear. By doing this inner practice, it will help us to process and purify.

I want to make a commentary on when the golden sphere shoots out. It is very important to be focused because you will probably see, if you have the vision and you're doing this prayer, that as you're going towards the star, you will tend to not go there. You will tend to veer off to the left or go into the center of the sun or [otherwise] not do it. You will tend to not do it because there is fear. There is fear of going through. This might be tied to fear of not wanting to come back. But [in any case] there is fear. And so you may need to practice just the pure attention of moving through. Then once you do go through, then it is a time of blessing and prasad. And sometimes teachings or healing gifts or healing energy is given to you in that space.

Now if you were dying and you were on your last breath, this is one yogic way of dying. Where your body is refined, you're ninety or whatever, ready to kick, and boom. You go out. You go up. You go through and you don't come back. This is one way to die. Okay? But just be sensitive to when it is time to come back, and *come back*. And follow those instructions including sharing of the gifts that you may have received there. And that whole image of covering this sphere—when I did it myself and I covered my sphere, I could feel that this sphere was hot and spinning. And when I held it, I could feel the warmth go through my body and heal my body. That is like a tantra. It is an image of a tantra, of the yin receiving the yang, cooling the yang down. And the yin is harmonized, or heated up by the yang, and then taken to a deeper, warmer place.

And I also want to say that there can be an addition to this [practice] where you can tie in the energy, for the women, of the ovaries up into the adrenals. You can build another power base so the [energy of the] left ovary can move up and be a support for the left kidney, and the [energy of the] right ovary for the right kidney, as a deeper base. Or, for the man, it can be the testicles.

And then you can also feel that bliss-line, too. The colors would be the same. I noticed when I was doing that exercise that I could feel that those areas of the second chakra were spontaneously wanting to hook in. So that is kind of an elaboration on that prayer. This is my commentary on the prayer at this time.

Howard, would you share the comments you made on the death of Jesus and the parallel universes?

HOWARD: The crucifixion and resurrection of Jesus proved the indestructibility and ultimate victory of the spirit; who we all are. Some people consider that to die as the body and resurrect as the spirit is the ultimate victory. Others believe that to allow the body to be killed, then to rise again with the body is the ultimate victory. Others still believe that to avoid the body's death even in the face of great odds, is victory. Still for others, it is the ultimate victory to take the body with you after death. If all of these versions, and others, are each enacted in parallel universes, then the gift of the knowledge of the eternal nature of spirit can be received by the greatest number of people, regardless of their personal belief systems. The revelation of this truth was of the greatest importance, not the scientific facts surrounding it.

ENDNOTES

1. Rudi (1928-1973) was also formally known as Swami Rudrananda. He was one of the first American-born Tantric kundalini yogis to teach in the United States (see bibliography). He served as Adi Da's first human Guru.

2. *Mary's Message to the World*, by Annie Kirkwood, is full of teachings and prophecies from Mother Mary. The book addresses many of the "Earth changes" that had initially been predicted for the mid-1990's. Mother Mary also discusses her life with Joseph, and other of her incarnations. (See bibliography.)

3. Prophecy is a difficult business. The real hope of prophecy is not to be correct 100 percent of the time, but to activate a change in action so as to *prevent* prophecy from being fulfilled. In this respect, the prophets of the Earth changes, including Annie Kirkwood, Gordon-Michael Scallion, Sun Bear, and Joya Pope were successful for the early part of the 1990s.

4. This digression into the most mundane of affairs probably surprised Solana the most, but in retrospect had a very positive impact on Chris's practical and spiritual life.

5. "Infinite Soul" is a term used in the Michael teachings. It means one who is fully and completely living as the Divine. They are extremely rare, and have great import. Examples are Krishna, Jesus, and Buddha. See Jose Stevens, Ph.D., and Simon Warwick-Smith, *The Michael Handbook*, pp. 54-55 (in bibliography).

6. The 11:11 was a worldwide event on January 11, 1992, that heralded the activation of a 20-year cycle involving the intensification of spiritual energies for Mother Earth and her people. Tens of thousands of people took part in ceremonies on that day, which especially involved the transmission of Archangelic energies. 11:11 is a cellular code anciently embedded in our soul structure for spiritual awakening. For more details, see *11:11*, by Solara (see bibiography).

7. Da is an ancient Sanskrit word for the Divine Person as "Giver."

8. The Gopis (pronounced go-peas) were the local young women who tended the cows in the fields near the area where Krishna meditated. They became enchanted with his radiance, and became his most ardent devotees. (See Swami Shivananda, *Lord Krishna*, in bibliography.)

9. Sai Baba of Shirdi (? – 1918) was one of the greatest saints near the turn of the century. He lived as a poor fakir in the Indian village of Shirdi (Maharastra state). He was worshipped by the Hindu and Muslim community alike. Countless miracles are credited to him. (See Mani Sahukar, *Sai Baba: The Saint of Shirdi*, in bibliography.)

10. Mother Meera (1960-) is an Indian Avatar of the Divine Mother who was born Self-Realized. She now lives and teaches in Thalheim, Germany, giving silent darshan to her devotees.

11. The Eighty-Four Mahasiddhas are the lineage of eighty-four Medieval Buddhist Masters who were all possessed of magical powers and displayed very unconventional behavior. They lived in India, Nepal, Tibet, and Indonesia. Their stories are told in Buddha's Lions by Abhayadatta (see bibliography).

12. See *The Michael Handbook*, pp.47, 64.

13. Swami Gurumayi Chidvilasananda (1955-) is a kundalini yogini who is the lineage successor to Swami Muktananda Paramahansa. She continues the work of her Siddha Yoga lineage, living and working primarily in India and the United States.

14. Adi Da (1939-) is an American Spiritual Master who teaches a new dharma based on *Radical Understanding*. He was born in a state of enlightenment, or the "Bright" as he describes it, paradoxically relinquishing it so as to live and function as a normal child, and then went through a spiritual process of full bodily realization of the "Bright" as an adult. Adi Da has written more than three dozen original spiritual works and created a new spiritual culture for students of his way. He is also called "Heart Master Da" and The Ruchira Buddha Adi Da Samraj.

15. Swami Muktananda Paramahansa (1908-1982) was a great Adept of kundalini yoga—the first prominent Indian yogi to bring the kundalini teachings to the United States on a large scale. He served as Guru to Gurumayi, Rudi, and Adi Da. (See bibliography.)

GLOSSARY

Tibetan words are indicated by (Tib.), Sanskrit words by (Skt.), Greek words by (Gk.), Latin words by (Lat.), and Chinese words by (Chin.).

Advaita Vedanta   (Skt.) Highest form of unqualified non-dualism, personified by Shankaracharya in his work *Viveka Chudamani* (*Crest Jewel of Discrimination*).

Agnus Dei   (Lat.) The Lamb of God, where the soul and God become one. A Christian conception of the "Guru."

Archangel Gabriel   Archangel of Divine Glory and Ecstasy, symbolized by a trumpet.

Archangel Melchizedek   Archangel of Divine Wisdom, symbolized by a sceptre.

Archangel Metatron   Archangel of Divine Love, symbolized by a shepherd's staff or crozier.

Archangel Michael (Mikael)   Archangel of Divine Power and Protection, symbolized by a sword.

Archangel Uriel   Archangel of Devotion, the Keeper of all prayers.

Bhajan   (Skt.) A form of devotional singing in India, best represented by the gopis' ecstatic singing for their beloved Lord Krishna.

Chakra   (Skt.) Literally "wheel." The chakras are the seven principal inner structures of the subtle body.

Chi

(Chin.) The life-force, or vital energy, that pervades all living things.

Christos

(Gk.) The universal energy of the Christ-Force.

Darshan

(Skt.) Literally "satsang with the truth," or "sitting at the feet of the spiritual master to receive blessings."

Devas

(Skt.) Literally "Gods," the deities that are the intercessors between man and God. Nature devas refers to the elemental spirits that fulfill God's work in Nature: the fairies, sprites, sylphs, and gnomes.

Dharma

(Skt.) A spiritual teaching or, more generally, the essence of right living and morality.

Dharmakaya

(Skt.) The truth-body of the Buddha; the absolute or cosmic body of the Guru.

Gelukpa Tradition

(Tib.) A Tibetan Buddhist lineage founded by Lama Tsongkapha. It was originally descended from the earlier New Kadam tradition founded by the Indian saint Atisha. It is known for its monastic scholarship and its connection with the Dalai Lama incarnations.

Guru

(Skt.) Spiritual preceptor or teacher. Literally, "one who removes all darkness."

Kali Yuga

(Skt.) Yuga is a time period of history as designated by the Hindu scriptures. Kali is usually associated with the Goddess Kali, the Dark Goddess of Hinduism. Some translate Kali Yuga as the Age of Darkness, others as the Age of Iron. According to Hindu scriptures, the current

age is the Kali Yuga because of the general
atheism and materialism of humanity.

Karma   (Skt.) Karma refers to the law of cause and
effect, the wheel of birth and death, which
perpetually recycles the soul from one incarnation to another.

Krishna   (Skt.) Krishna the Avatar, the great enlightened
teacher of Vedic India, reputedly appeared in
India approximately five thousand years ago.
Krishna was a prince and warrior, enlightened from birth, and the performer of countless miracles. His conversations with his friend
and devotee, Arjuna, are the basis for the
Bhagavad Gita.

Kundalini   (Skt.) Typically described as the spirit or "energy"
that lies dormant at the base of the spine
until spiritual awakening occurs, when it ascends
up the spinal line to the brain core and above.
Adi Da further explains that the kundalini is
never truly dormant, only greatly suppressed;
and that it also involves the descending aspect
of spiritual energy that moves down the frontal
line of the body until it reaches the base of
the spine.

Mahashakti   (Skt.) Shakti is defined as spiritual energy.
Mahashakti refers to the Goddess-Power as
Divine Spiritual Energy that pervades the cosmos.

Milarepa   An eleventh-century Tibetan yogi-saint who
was well-known for his arduous spiritual
practice under his teacher, the Guru Marpa.

Medjugorje   A village in Hercegovina (formerly a part of

Yugoslavia) where a manifestation of Mother Mary first appeared to several children in 1981. Medjugorje has become a major pilgrimage site, and many have testified to remarkable spiritual occurrences there.

Morning Star   An esoteric portal that can be seen in mystical visions. It appears as a star or a setting sun.

Nirvana   (Skt.) The great "quenching," the state of enlightenment in Buddhism.

Noösphere   A word coined by Teilhard de Chardin (1881-1955), a French Catholic paleontologist, to describe a layer of atmosphere composed of the collective consciousness of mankind.

Order of the Lamb   An esoteric order of healers and priests who specifically work with the vibration of Archangel Metatron.

Order of Melchizedek   An esoteric order of healers and priests who specifically work with the vibration of Archangel Melchizedek.

Parama   Parama is a subtle energy vortex located in the Amazon jungle of Brazil. It is used in the Umbanda shamanic tradition as an activation for healing the chi, or "green" vibration of energy in the body.

Prasad   (Skt.) Typically refers to sacrificial offerings of food or flowers made to a Divinity or Guru, which are then blessed and returned to the devotees as a spiritual gift.

Rishi   (Skt.) A seer of truth. According to Hindu

scripture, there were seven rishis who created and maintained the universe.

Samadhi (Skt.) A state of oneness in which the sense of the world is suspended and one feels bliss. There are many kinds of samadhi, ranging from initial and temporary absorption to permanent realization of Divine Union.

Samsara (Skt.) The world as it is ordinarily perceived —the unenlightened world viewed by an unenlightened person.

Sananda Another name for the cosmic person of Christ.

Shabd Yoga (Skt.) A yoga of absorption into the subtle sounds and lights above the body. The Sant lineage of Pakistan is a primary lineage-holder of this teaching.

Shiva (Skt.) Sometimes considered the Destroyer part of the Hindu Trinity, and sometimes as the Divine and Transcendental Consciousness. Shiva is typically depicted meditating on a tiger's skin, with a cobra wrapped around his neck, and carrying a trident.

Shivaite A devotee or worshipper of Shiva. It is estimated that there are at least two hundred million Shivaites in the world today.

Spiritus Aeternus (Lat.) The Eternal Spirit.

Tangka (Tib.) Typically a spiritual painting of Deities or Gurus, on a silk scroll.

Tantra (Skt.) The word tantra has many definitions.

Here it is used to describe a spiritual practice in which the masculine (yang) and the feminine (yin) aspects of the body-mind are harmonized to create a deeper balance that sustains further spiritual evolution.

Umbanda   A Brazilian shamanic tradition still in practice today.

Vedic Time   The period from approximately 5000 BC to 1500 BC in India, when a great oral tradition was kept alive by the brahmin priests. This tradition eventually was recorded as the Vedas, which are the essential spiritual teachings of Hinduism. There are four Vedas: Rig, Sama, Yajur, and Atharva. The ancient Vedic Time is considered by Indians as the apex of India's spiritual glory.

Vishnu   (Skt.) Part of the Hindu Trinity, along with Shiva and Brahma. Vishnu is the sustainer aspect of God.

Yang   (Chin.) A Taoist word that describes an activity or object that has the attributes of heat, focus, intensity, and penetration. Often synonymous with the masculine. Yang is paired with yin.

Yin   (Chin.) A Taoist word that describes an activity or object that has the attributes of coolness, moisture, inwardness, and diffusion. Often synonymous with the feminine. Yin is paired with yang.

BIBLIOGRAPHY

Abhayadatta (translated by James B. Robinson), *Buddha's Lions: The Lives of the Eighty-Four Siddhas*. Berkeley, CA: Dharma Publishing, 1979.

Adi Da, *The Heart's Shout*. Middletown, CA: The Dawn Horse Press, 1996.

Ashton, Joan, *The People's Madonna*. London: Fount Paperbacks (Harper Collins), 1991. (This book is an excellent introduction to the story of the appearances of Mother Mary at Medjugorje.)

Bubba Free John (Adi Da), *The Enlightenment of the Whole Body*. Middletown, CA: The Dawn Horse Press, 1978. (See page 445 for a superb, contemporary analysis of Jesus and the Morning Star.)

Da Free John (Adi Da), *The Fire Gospel*. Middletown, CA: The Dawn Horse Press, 1982.

De Montfort, St. Louis-Marie Grignon, *True Devotion to the Blessed Virgin*. Langley Bucks, England: St. Paul Publications, 1982.

Fuller, John G., *Edgar Cayce*. New York: Warner Books, 1989.

Gurumayi Chidvilasananda, *Kindle My Heart* (Vols. I & II). South Fallsburg, NY: SYDA Foundation, 1989.

Kirkwood, Annie, *Mary's Message to the World*. New York: Pedigree Books, 1991.

Mann, A.T., *Millennium Prophecies*. Rockport, MA: Element Books, 1992.

Mother Meera, *Answers*. Ithaca, NY: Meeramman, 1991.

Muktananda, Swami, *The Play of Consciousness*. South Fallsburg, NY: SYDA Foundation, 1971.

New Testament with Old Testament References. La Habra, CA: The Lockman Foundation, 1960.

Rudi (Swami Rudrananda), *Spiritual Cannibalism*. Cambridge, MA: Rudra Press, 1987.

Sahukar, Mani, *Sai Baba: The Saint of Shirdi*. San Francisco: The Dawn Horse Press, 1977.

Sanchez-Ventura Y Pascual, F., *The Apparitions of Garabandal*. Detroit, MI: San Miguel Publishing Co., 1967.

Shivananda, Swami, *Lord Krishna*. Tehri-Garhwal, India: Divine Life Society, 1990.

Solara, *11:11*. Charlottesville, VA: Star-Borne Unlimited, 1992.

Stevens, Ph.D., Jose, and Simon Warwick-Smith, *The Michael Handbook*. Sonoma, CA: Warwick Press, 1990. (This book contains an excellent overview of the teachings of the Causal Plane guide known as Michael.)

ACKNOWLEDGEMENTS

My first acknowledgement is to my spiritual teachers who some-
how found a reason to teach and bless a worldly person such as
myself. They are Adi Da, Ammachi, and Mother Meera. Adi Da
has been my first and primary teacher, and I have been greatly
influenced by his teachings and spiritual blessings. Sometimes
in this text, words or phrases I learned from his teachings were
used by me that were too incidental to be footnoted, but may
be recognized by his students and devotees as coming from his
usage of them. I suggest that any serious spiritual practitioner
familiarize themselves with the marvelous and rich written
dharma that Sri Adi Da has created. I feel it is a great treasure.
Ammachi and Mother Meera have primarily taught me in
silence, and have been a great source of love and guidance for
me in the last seven years.

Having been taught (and molded) by them to be more perceptive,
I was able to receive the blessed teachings of Mother Mary, who
has my eternal gratitude, and also to receive the vision of the
Blessed Archangels, who I thank for their unfathomably wonderful
spiritual service and teachings.

I wish to thank those friends who came to each of the discourses
and contributed to bringing the teachings down to earth: Lia, Shelley,
Howard, Chris, Mitchell, Devaka, Fritz, Roxanne, Lance, Annie,
and Karaina.

This production of the book was made possible by the efforts of
five people. Larry Boggs performed his usual brilliant editing to
make the text readable and grammatically correct. Lynn Magers
transcribed the audiotapes and helped with her Bible expertise and
good cheer. Mitchell Saunders used his extensive spiritual and academic
background to be of tremendous help in preparing the glossary.
Finally, Leslie Waltzer and Micah Johnson of Crowfoot Design
Group, created a beautiful book cover and design for the book.

ABOUT SOLANA

Solana joined an ashram community directly out of university and did spiritual practice there until his mid-thirties. Upon leaving the confines of community spiritual practice, he continued his spiritual process under the guidance of other teachers.

Mother Mary first appeared to him in 1979 when She revealed Herself in Her Dharmakhaya or Transcendental Form. Thereafter, She would occasionally appear in times of Solana's spiritual need.

In 1989, Solana began to have visions of the Archangels, starting with Archangel Michael, and later with Archangel Melchizedek and Archangel Metatron. Starting in 1991, with the advent of the 11:11 event, Solana began to facilitate angel and archangel meditations. A special aspect of this work is the leading of empowerment ceremonies for the archangels Michael, Metatron, and Melchizedek.

He currently runs a small consulting business and lives in Northern California.

MORE INFORMATION

Solana can be reached through BLUE COUGAR PRESS if there are any groups of people interested in direct instruction in the prayers contained herein. Enquiries are especially welcomed from Europe, as Solana travels there regularly.

Blue Cougar Press invites your correspondence and comments about *The Cosmic Christ.*

Write to:

BLUE COUGAR PRESS
P.O. Box 2216
San Rafael, CA 94912
USA
FAX (415) 455-8185

Copies of *The Cosmic Christ* may be ordered directly from the publisher for US $14.00 ($12.50 and $1.50 postage). California residents please add 7.25% sales tax.

Hear the discourses as they were first heard on a set of seven audiotapes. Listening to the audiotapes offers a profound opportunity to experience the transmissions and activations as they were given. Price is US $45.00 ($42.00 and $3.00 for US priority mail). California residents please add 7.25% sales tax. Foreign shipments extra. Make checks payable to BLUE COUGAR PRESS, and order through the mail at the above address. (The audiotapes are available only as a complete set.)

Ave Maria